THE AMERICAN SOLDIER IN FICTION, 1880–1963

THE AMERICAN
1880–1963: A HISTORY
WARFARE AND
ESTABLISHMENT

Iowa State University Press / Ames

SOLDIER IN FICTION,
OF ATTITUDES TOWARD
THE MILITARY

Peter Aichinger

1 9 7 5

PS
374
M5
A4

5/1976
Am. Lit.

PETER AICHINGER, chairman of the department of English, Collège militaire royal de Saint-Jean, was educated at the universities of Toronto, Ottawa, and Sussex. He holds a doctoral degree in literature (Sussex) and teaches in his primary field of interest, modern American literature. He served with the Royal Canadian Horse Artillery in northwest Europe and has lived in Germany, 1960–1962, and in England, 1968–1970.

© 1975 The Iowa State University Press
Ames, Iowa 50010. All rights reserved
Composed and printed by
The Iowa State University Press
First edition, 1975
International Standard Book Number: 0-8138-0100-1

Library of Congress Cataloging in Publication Data

Aichinger, Peter, 1933–
    The American solder in fiction, 1880–1963.

    Bibliography: p.
    1. American fiction—20th century—History with criticism. 2. American fiction—19th century—History and criticism. 3. Militarism—United States. 4. War in literature. 5. War and literature. I. Title.

PS374.M5A4   813'.03   75–14494
ISBN 0-8138-0100-1

CONTENTS

PREFACE

This work constitutes an examination of the attitudes toward warfare and the military establishment that can be detected in a representative number of the war novels written by American authors in the period from 1880 to 1963. It is not intended to be primarily a work of literary criticism, although some observations on the literary merits of various works have been made in passing. The principal object of the book has been to discuss the American war novels in relation to historical, economic, and political events that accompanied or preceded their appearance, in order to be able to observe the attitudes that seem to be peculiar to the citizens of the United States and to describe the changes those attitudes have undergone in the last eighty years. The time span has been divided into four main segments— 1880–1917, 1917–1939, 1939–1952, and 1953–1963—corresponding to what are felt to be major epochs in the American experience of warfare; each section reviews the more important events contributing to the American outlook on war or the military establishment in that period and discusses the war literature produced during the period.

Perhaps the most important reason for undertaking this study was my belief in the archetypal importance of warfare as a literary theme, not only in the United States but in all countries and at all times. In our own time one sees the battles of World War I and World War II fought and refought in every medium from pulp magazine to film. If it is truly said that "boy meets girl" is the most popular theme ever devised, then it can also be said that "men in arms" runs a close second. It is a curious fact, however, that although the critics have dealt at length with the manifestations of love interest in literature, they have given only sporadic attention to the theme of warfare. Lately some studies of this subject have appeared, but one is still hard pressed to find a first-class full-length study of the American war novel comparable to, say, Bernard Bergonzi's treatment of the World War I British war novel in *Heroes' Twilight*.

I believe that warfare merits serious study as a theme in literature in general, and especially so in the case of the literature of the

United States. First of all, the United States is the most powerful nation in the world, possessing a military machine whose scope and capabilities rank with the wonders of the modern world. Secondly, aside from the United States' military establishment per se as a dominant factor in world affairs, one is intrigued by a peculiarly American mentality governing the use of force. President Kennedy was aware that his nation was "entrapped in an ethos of violence,"[1] a point made only too clear by his own tragic end. America is, after all, only very recently removed from the time when violence was the quick and simple solution to the problems of the pioneers; in some parts of the United States this frontier mentality still exists. Everywhere it lends a peculiar color and tone to American war literature.

There are studies, like W. M. Frohock's *The Novel of Violence in America,* that deal with the element of violence in American letters as a whole. My book is restricted to a discussion of those novels which have as their theme the organized violence known as warfare. Thus where Frohock's book, for example, discusses some novels—like *Three Soldiers, For Whom the Bell Tolls,* and *A Farewell to Arms*—with which I also deal, his chief interest centers on novelists like Thomas Wolfe, James T. Farrell, and Erskine Caldwell—all of whom are irrelevant to my study. Yet the sort of violence of which he writes—i.e., the barbarism and impetuosity characteristic of American life—is not unrelated to the more organized violence of warfare: James T. Farrell's Studs Lonigan is not greatly different in terms of personality from James Gould Cozzens's Colonel Benny Carricker.

I have tried to suggest some of the reasons for the essential unity of violence in American letters. It has been noted that the American Revolution engendered a certain lack of respect for due process of law. This tendency was fortified by the exigencies of frontier life: the process of wresting land from its rightful owners or of settling boundary disputes with France and Mexico did not always permit the moral niceties to be observed. As General U. S. Grant said of the Mexican War, in which he served with distinction, "It was one of the most unjust ever waged by a stronger against a weaker nation."[2] At the same time, the men who performed these tasks necessarily became heroes in the eyes of the nation. Thus many an American folk hero—Davy Crockett, John Mosby, even John Brown—was a thug whose actions were legitimized because he fought in what appeared to be a good cause. The defenders of the Alamo, almost all of whom were adventurers, became "soldiers" in the national mind.

In this book I have argued that the real connection between the war novel and the novel of violence in America began to manifest itself in those works written toward the end of the nineteenth century. Up to that time almost no war novels of enduring interest had been written: James Fenimore Cooper is not remembered for *The Spy* (1821); of the hundreds of novels written about the Civil War, perhaps one remembers De Forest's *Miss Ravenel's Conversion* (1867). In the United States the great tide of war novels began sometime after 1890 with the publication of Stephen Crane's *The Red Badge of Courage* (1895), Herman Melville's *Billy Budd* (written c. 1888, published 1924), and Ambrose Bierce's *Tales of Soldiers and Civilians* (1891). That is to say, the war novel began to appear at a time when the frontier as a locus of violence had disappeared. This suggests that warfare, at least as it was treated in fiction, was a new avatar of the American spirit of violence; the soldier came to replace the cowboy or the frontiersman in the popular imagination.

I have also noted some of the other factors contributing to the rise of the American war novel at the end of the nineteenth century. For one thing, the increasing complexities of international relations tended to involve the United States in more and more serious foreign engagements. The Spanish-American War served as an introduction to the shattering events of World War I and World War II, which in turn gave way to the cold war, Korea, and Viet Nam. At the same time the "military establishment" began to emerge as a recognizable entity, starting with the efforts of Elihu Root and the perfection of the General Staff system in the period from 1894 to 1901. During the twentieth century the military establishment has come increasingly to have a form and existence of its own and to play an important part in the affairs of the nation. The attitude of American writers toward this element in the national life is therefore necessarily a phenomenon of the twentieth century.

Having argued that the disappearance of the frontier, a larger involvement in foreign wars, and the rise of the military establishment as a separate entity all contributed to the emergence of the war novel as an identifiable genre in the period after 1880, I suggest that a new dimension of awareness has opened in the years since 1945. For example, there is the question raised by Arnold Toynbee as to why the United States has been forced out of its traditional isolationism and neutrality by Russian aggressiveness, when Hitler's aggressiveness and the Kaiser's did not particularly impress her. To Toynbee the Russian threat is less great in real terms than the German one ever was. He tries to explain the American reaction in part as rancor at Russian perfidy over lend-lease agreements.[3] The truth probably is that before Hiroshima the Americans could never believe that anyone was able to muster more military and industrial force than they could. This seems to have become the real and enduring significance of the atomic bomb: not that it ended the war with Japan (the arguments in favor of its use both before and after the event all have a strangely academic quality) but that it awakened the Americans to the fact of their own peril.[4] Thus the period from about 1880 to about 1960 seems to form a historical unit in which one can observe the development of certain related literary themes and historical events.

Within this time framework, the purpose of this book is to indicate some of the ways in which the American war novels have reflected the attitude of the American people toward warfare and the military establishment. It seems possible to show that in the period before the nation actually went to war against a major external enemy the novels were objective and idealistic; after World War I the novels reflected the horror and chagrin of a people who had tasted combat for the first time; the novels of World War II reveal a different concept of war—more sophisticated and less idealistic—and treat a different set of problems than those of World War I; and in the period after the Korean War, in keeping with the completely altered nature of warfare itself, the war novelists have adopted a point of view that suggests a new attitude toward warfare on the part of the American people. In other words, the American war novel tends to bear out Daniel Boorstin's contention: "What a nation means by war or peace is as characteristic of its experience and as intimately involved with all its other ways as are its laws or its religion."[5]

I would define the term "war novel" as any long work of prose fiction in which the lives and actions of the characters are principally affected by warfare or the military establishment. By this definition E. E. Cummings's *The Enormous Room,* in which the main characters are all civilians, is very much a war novel; Carson McCullers's *Reflections in a Golden Eye,* in which the protagonists are all in the Army, is not. In the former work war is the primordial fact dominating the lives of all the characters, while in the latter the Army merely provides a certain social structure necessary to the working out of the plot; another setting—a Georgia plantation for example—would have served as well.

Furthermore, there is a strong tendency in war literature for memoirs and works of reminiscence to encroach upon the field of pure fiction. It is impossible to clearly separate works like *The Enormous Room* or Robert Graves's *Goodbye to All That,* which are based on factual experiences, from novels such as Leon Uris's *Battle Cry* that are ostensibly fictitious. The whole problem is further complicated by the rise of works of reportage which overlap areas of both memoir and fiction. John Hersey's *Hiroshima* and

William Bradford Huie's *The Execution of Private Slovik* are only two of the works that fall into this category. To separate these various works into rigid categories would be exceedingly difficult and serve no purpose.

From this it can be seen that the term "war novel" is a rather loose one; yet it permits a degree of flexibility that is very useful in dealing with war literature as a whole. Also, there seems to be an instinctive comprehension of what the term stands for; most critics use it without apology or further explanation, on the assumption that the reference is clear. In fact, attempts to refine the term usually only lead to greater confusion. Leslie Fiedler, for example, in *Waiting for the End,* decided to call these works "antiwar novels" because of the strong element of protest characteristic of many of the novels written after World War I. His term serves only to becloud the issue, because there is actually a whole series of American novels about World War I that could more accurately be called "prowar novels." For all of these reasons, therefore, it seems best simply to accept the fact that the term "war novel" designates a fairly diversified body of literature, but there is no real disagreement over the extent of that body. On the strength of this argument I have included at least passing mention of the works of Ambrose Bierce in the Introduction to this book. To ignore Bierce's stories on the ground that they are not novels would be mere quibbling: Bierce himself defined a novel as "a short story padded." He is perhaps the most important writer to have served for any considerable length of time in the Civil War, and to disregard his work entirely would be a serious defect in a study of this kind.

Fundamental to my approach to this study is the idea that literature may be beneficially examined as one of many components of national life, all of which interact with each other: i.e., it is important to discuss works of literature in relation to the historical, economic, and political events that accompanied or preceded their appearance on the scene. If one accepts this premise, then one must also accept its corollary: that a legitimate study of this type need not, in fact cannot, be a sweeping examination of a literary theme. That is to say, it is valid and important to examine some literary works in relation to some important national events rather than offer an exhaustive and purely literary discussion of all the manifestations of the theme of war in American literature. The full title of this study—*The American Soldier in Fiction, 1880-1963: A History of Attitudes toward Warfare and the Military Establishment*—has been chosen with this point in mind. I was more interested in examining the manner in which novels revealed a set of attitudes than in writing a work of literary criticism.

It should be established that the selection of works to be discussed must be more or less arbitrary, based on my instinct for what is important to my argument. Instinct seems to be the best guide, because no satisfactory literary criteria exist by which to judge the works that are suitable to this study. Nor does the sheer volume of war literature really constitute a serious problem. Of the hundreds, perhaps thousands, of war novels written since 1880, only a very few have earned a permanent place in the nation's literature; the same titles keep reappearing in literary articles, reviews, and contemporary histories. As Norman Mailer has observed, "War is as full of handbooks as engineering, but it is more of a mystery, and the mystery is what separates the great war novels from the good ones."[6] For example, few people would deny that *From Here to Eternity* is a technically inferior novel: verbose, overly long, the story sensational and in places naive, and many of the characters stereotyped and two-dimensional. Yet like *The Naked and the Dead*—another American novel which shares some of the same defects—it has the ring of truth, the quality of accurately rendering a significant experience in a manner that has appealed to an enormous number of Americans. Therefore it is included, while some technically and imaginatively superior works may be ignored.

ACKNOWLEDGEMENTS

I was guided in the writing of this book by Professor Marcus Cunliffe of the University of Sussex, for whose patience and kindness I am extremely grateful.

My thanks are also due to the authorities of le Collège militaire royal de Saint-Jean, who made it possible for me take leave with pay while I was working on this book, and to the Department of National Defence of Canada for other forms of assistance.

While my research was in progress I was assisted by the librarians of the following institutions: le Collège militaire royal, the Royal Military College of Canada, the National Library of Canada, the Library of Congress, the University of Sussex, the British Museum, and the Wiener Library in London.

This book has been published with the help of a grant from the Humanities Research Council of Canada, using funds provided by the Canada Council.

INTRODUCTION: 1880–1917

If one considers that the United States began to be fully aware of itself as a nation in the period after 1880 and that its military establishment was thereafter representative of the nation as a whole (i.e., it was drawn from all parts of the country and its efforts were directed against common external enemies), it seems reasonable to inquire into the principal characteristics of the American military establishment in the period before World War I and to establish to what extent these facets were reflected in American literature.

It is possible to delineate five main characteristics: pragmatism, a "team" syndrome, a persistent democratic-aristocratic tension, idealism, and a general lack of experience and psychological preparation for combat. Some of these elements, especially pragmatism and the team mentality, persist to the present day; the others have undergone a process of mutation or have disappeared entirely. From the outset, however, they were dominant factors both in the military establishment and in the civilian attitude toward that organization; wherever writers rendered the military experience in fiction, these same elements seem to shape the author's treatment of their theme.

In contrast to the European emphasis on ceremony and tradition in military life, the United States Army from its inception was based on a philosophy of pragmatism. Emphasis was on the immediately useful and practical. When the native American militia tended to be undisciplined and to show a disastrous tendency to concern themselves more with the gathering of their crops than with the fighting of battles, the Americans had no qualms about importing a German officer to help reorganize the army in the winter of 1777. Unhampered by the weight of tradition and faced with the alternatives of victory or destruction, they turned to men who could teach them to function efficiently. Names like Von Steuben, Lafayette, Kosciusko, and de Kalb may have rung strangely upon the colonial ear, but the soldiers overcame their resentment of the foreigners when they recognized the primordial quality of know-how.[1] To this was added a further dimension of pragmatism in that the Americans adopted tactics peculiarly suited to skirmishing in the wilderness; they also shot to kill, whereas the European soldier tended to "fire mechanically in the general direction of the enemy."[2] The Revolution, then, committed the Americans to following the well-established European habit of solving problems by force of arms; in other words, it marked the point at which the frontier tradition of violence became institutionalized. At the same time it reinforced the native American habit of cutting across traditional modes of action to find the most efficient method of operation.

In the same vein, in the nineteenth century the establishment of a military academy—long anathema to the public mind—could be rationalized by the fact that it was intended to train artillery and engineer officers. Both corps based their studies to a great extent on the useful sciences of mathematics, surveying, physics, and chemistry: "[The institution's] principal object was to produce engineers for military and civil employment. It was the equivalent of the École Polytechnique, not of St. Cyr: a technical institute designed to serve the entire nation as a practical scientific school, not a professional academy for the military vocation."[3] In most armies of the world the elite corps are the cavalry and the horse artillery; in the United States the Corps of Engineers is and has always been the *corps d'élite*.

The pragmatic attitude toward warfare has not been confined to military organizations alone. When the Spanish-American War broke out, the ancient idea of legitimized piracy was revived as a means of turning warfare into a profitable business. "An enterprising gentleman of Norfolk, 'representing a party of capitalists who are enthusiastic supporters of the Government' . . . applied to the State Department for a letter of marque 'to enable us to lawfully capture Spanish merchant vessels and torpedo boats,' adding: 'We have secured option on a fine steam vessel, and on receipt of proper documents will put to sea forthwith.' "[4] The remainder of the business community, with the exception of the press, saw the war as a financial disaster. With a practicality equal to that of "the enterprising gentleman of Norfolk" they suggested buying Cuba instead of fighting for it. It had been rumored that Spain was willing to sell Cuba, and the *Wall Street Journal* suggested that $200,000,000 or even $250,000,000 could be found to purchase the island—a bargain considering that those firms trading with Cuba estimated that they lost $100,000,000 per year as a result of the war, or $300,000,000 by 1898.[5]

A further and much more peculiarly American extension of this concept of war as pragmatic private enterprise is revealed in the persistent belief that a mechanical device could be invented to eliminate the elements of danger and personal contact from warfare. In a review of Captain Mahan's *The Influence of Seapower upon History*, Theodore Roosevelt once said, "In the event of a European contest, it is not likely that we should be allowed [four weeks] before the fatal blow fell. There is a loose popular idea that we could defend ourselves by some kind of patent method, invented on the spur of the moment. This is sheer folly. There is no doubt that American ingenuity could do something, but not enough."[6] The vehemence of his rebuttal, even the fact that he saw it necessary to comment on this "loose popular idea," is evidence of the hold it had on the popular imagination. Nor is it surprising to find this mentality in America. In a society whose natural genius turned spontaneously to reducing such messy tasks as coal mining and oil refining to operations capable of being accomplished by a handful of white-smocked technicians seated in air-conditioned control rooms, war was only another problem that had best be solved in terms of cost accounting, time-and-motion study, and avoidance of loss due to employee fatalities.

When Roosevelt spoke out against the push-button approach to war, he may have been thinking of a wry little novel called *The Great War Syndicate*, published the year before by Frank Stockton. This book deals with a naval war in the late nineteenth century between the United States and Great Britain, which is resolved by farming the United States' defense commitment out to a "war syndicate" which proceeds to win the war by inventing and using "crabs" (submersibles capable of ripping rudders out of ships) and "repellers" (spring-armored ships armed with "instantaneous motor bombs" having approximately the effect of nuclear weapons but capable of being fired with great accuracy and no radioactive fallout). Only one man is killed in the entire war, and that because a derrick accidentally falls on him.

We see the same belief in gadgetry as a means of achieving a quick and painless victory in Mark Twain's *A Connecticut Yankee in King Arthur's Court* (1889). The Yankee stays ahead of his enemies by establishing telephone communications with a friend at court; when he is challenged to a joust, he employs a lasso and a revolver to defeat his opponents. Finally, in a horrible parody of the *Götterdämmerung*, he slaughters his enemies en masse as the iron-clad knights press forward unwittingly against highly charged electric fences and into range of his machine guns. It is this same marriage of grisly humor and basic pragmatism that underlies Milo Minderbinder's contract bombing of his own air base in Joseph Heller's *Catch-22* (1962):

His crews spared the landing strip and the mess halls so that they could land safely when their work was done and enjoy a hot snack before retiring. They bombed with their landing lights on, since no one was shooting back. They bombed all four squadrons, the officers' club and the Group Headquarters building. Men bolted from their tents in sheer terror and did not know in which direction to turn. Wounded soon lay screaming everywhere. A cluster of fragmentation bombs exploded in the yard of the officers' club and punched jagged holes in the side of the building and in the bellies and backs of a row of lieutenants and captains standing at the bar. They doubled over in agony and dropped. . . . Decent people everywhere were affronted, and Milo was all washed up until he opened his books to the public and disclosed the tremendous profit he had made.[7]

Twain's work may reveal a neurotic enjoyment of slaughter, Stockton's tongue is certainly in his cheek, Heller is working in the realm of black humor; but in all three cases their buffoonery depends on a parody of the characteristic American pragmatism. The fundamental accuracy of their insight is attested by Henry Adams's comment that during the War of 1812, "the British complained as a grievance that the Americans adopted new and unwarranted devices in naval warfare; that their vessels were heavier and better constructed, and their missiles of unusual shape and improper use."[8]

The "team" syndrome is directly related to this American pragmatism. The American characteristically views any problem in terms of mass production: reduce the problem to its component parts; make the parts interchangeable; find the most efficient means of mass-producing them; apply standardized methods of packaging, distribution, and advertising; and the problem is solved. Using this approach one can swamp the market with cars, soapflakes, hula hoops, or soldiers. The key to the system lies in the fact that the parts must be interchangeable. In human terms this means that friction must be reduced, personalities must not clash, cooperation is at a premium.

If Elihu Root and General Wood were responsible for consciously shaping the army as a machine with interchangeable parts, one can also say that American society as a whole tends to foster the team spirit by many factors. Perhaps the most important of these derives from John Dewey's very influential theory of education: "Since that part of the environment consisting of other persons is in many ways the most important part, much of the child's education would consist of experiments in cooperating with his kind." This factor also reveals itself in the American passion for team sports. Football, hockey, baseball, and basketball share the common element of requiring a certain number of players to submit themselves unquestioningly to the guidance of a coach, who is responsible for training the team and manipulating it to victory. The difference between these sports and the European favorite, soccer, is that the soccer team manager seems to have an administrative rather than an operational role; he has relatively little influence on the actual playing of the game, whereas in America the coach can (and often does) direct every single move in a highly complex operation. In fact, one thinks of the team as an extension of the manager; one says, "Vince Lombardi won fourteen games that season" just as one says, "Eisenhower won n . . . battles in his career as a soldier."

Robert Sherwood has said that the American people are mentally conditioned to look to the "coach" for instructions and guidance when the going gets rough,[9] and in the armed forces this mentality has given rise to an interesting situation. The "team" generally consists of draftees, while the "coach" is usually a professional soldier; in the case of an officer he is usually a graduate of a military academy. On the one hand the American soldier is vitally conscious of his essentially civilian status and of the fact that the military is normally subject to civilian control. Added to this is the long history of ingrained antipathy toward professional soldiers whose chief occupations in the period from 1865 to 1898 were policing Congress's carpetbagging reconstruction policy in the South and killing Indians and more recently were maintaining order in labor disputes.[10] On the other hand there exists an innate admiration for the professional, the team captain, the coach.

Within certain limits then, the American responds instinctively to the demands of the team, and American war literature is colored throughout by variations on the team philosophy and the love-hate relationship with the professional soldier.[11] John Dos Passos's three soldiers are servile or defiant in the presence of authority, but they recognize their own comparative incompetence. E. E. Cummings's tone in *The Enormous Room* (1922) is very much that of the spectator; in fact the tone of sophomoric wisecracking almost succeeds in concealing the author's profoundly personal reaction to the war. For Lieutenant Henry in Hemingway's *A Farewell to Arms* (1929), the debacle at Caporetto and the subsequent panic-stricken conduct of the Italian officers reveal to him that he has made a mistake; the coach is incompetent, the team is disorganized, and therefore he is free to detach himself from it. Queeg in *The Caine Mutiny* (1951) and Melville Goodwin in John Marquand's novel lapse habitually into the jargon of the team, the coach, the playing field. Prewitt, in *From Here to Eternity* (1951), will tolerate almost any amount of goading by Master Sergeant Warden because Warden is the pro and makes no mistakes. In *The Thin Red Line* (1962) the reserve Captain Stein—who is otherwise intelligent, stable, and humane—falls into a state of forelock-tugging funk when the regimental commander speaks to him: " 'Magnificent, Stein, magnificent.' . . . Stein had a vivid mental picture of Colonel Tall's close-cropped, boyish, Anglo-Saxon head and un-lined, Anglo-Saxon face. . . . Stein pressed the button, managed a weak 'Yes, Sir. Over,' and released the button. He could not think of anything else to say."[12] At this point Stein has just lost a con-siderable number of men and faces a murderous fire from hidden Japanese positions. The situation is rendered even more incongru-ous by the fact that Colonel Tall is urging Stein and his men to go out and get killed in order that Tall may make a good showing before a visiting admiral.

Actually the root of the basic tension that exists between officer and enlisted man in the United States' forces is embedded in the character and organization of the country itself. In 1840 Tocqueville observed that in an aristocratic society being an of-ficer is partly a pastime, partly a duty, but the officer's social rank more or less fixes his military rank. Thus the private soldier does not dream of becoming an officer; whereas in a democratic society everyone can aspire to officer rank.[13] Theoretically the American soldier should never have resented the professional officer, since that officer should have been a common man raised to eminence by his own efforts. But the domination of the upper grades of the service by graduates of the service academies created a de facto aristocratic situation which the common soldier sensed and which aroused deep anxieties reaching back to the days of the Revolution. The colonists, lacking a military caste and the tradition of mili-tary "honor," had tended to be selfish and materialistic; unselfish service as officers held no special attraction for them, and the con-cepts of military honor and behavior as officers had to be intro-duced artificially by Washington.[14]

The officers of the well-trained, regular, more or less profes-sional army to which Washington had recourse during the war toyed with the idea of a coup while the colonies were awaiting a settlement after Yorktown,[15] an idea that aligned them against the farmers and militiamen. It was all very well that the coup never took place and that as late as 1917, Harry S. Truman could be *elected* first lieutenant of Battery F in the Second Missouri Field Artillery by a democratic vote of his fellow soldiers.[16] The distrust-ful equation of high military rank with aristocratic tendencies re-mained in the American mind; it is only the atomic bomb with its influence on every aspect of military life that has suceeded in modifying this situation in our own time.

If the American attitude toward warfare and the military es-tablishment before 1917 reflected a native pragmatism, paradoxi-cally it was also highly idealistic. *Gone with the Wind* (1936) has earned a permanent place in the history of American entertainment by expressing an important part of the national mythos: what Robert A. Lively has called "the myth of a war ruled by ante-bellum courtesies rather than military necessity" through which "we arrive at the scene of that frequently described war which was conducted with the formality of a duel, within the blood-lines of gigantic families."[17] One senses that the desire which underlay this myth sprang from an awareness of the crudity and harshness of frontier life as contrasted with European sophistication. Americans too could fight like gentlemen, and perhaps even teach the Euro-peans a lesson on the subject. As one Civil War officer put it, "This war is not one between mere military machines as soldiers are in Europe, but of rational thinking beings, fighting with the highest of motives on our side, and with the belief that theirs is the highest of motives on the part of the enemy."[18] The same tone of altruism and high purpose suffuses a letter from Captain Daniel McCook, Assistant Adjutant General in the Second Division (Union) at Shiloh:

As we passed through the orchard, lying with his shoulders propped against a peach-tree, I saw the mangled form of one of my best-loved classmates dressed in rebel uniform. . . . A smile beautified his features, while his eyes seemed gazing far to the southward, as if there an anxious mother were waiting for words of hope from that war-swept field. A cannon-ball had partly severed a branch of the tree. Flower-laden, it fell in scarlet festoons about his head—a fitting pall for his gallant, pure-hearted, yet erring nature.[19]

In crossing the Atlantic, warfare had undergone a sea change. It had regained an Arthurian chivalry; it was a family affair; it was outside of and superior to the political and economic broils, the chicanery that disfigured European wars. Even in a society com-mitted wholeheartedly to the production-line technique of solving problems, the machine image had to be soft-pedaled. In a speech in Chicago in October 1899, Elihu Root had referred to the Ameri-can soldier as a part of a machine; but, in the words of Walter Millis in 1956, "The idea that the American soldier was simply a cog in a 'great machine' was by no means as acceptable in 1899 as it has become to-day. For many, war was still a matter of young men 'springing to arms' and fighting the issue out with bullet, butt and bayonet in a deadly personal encounter."[20]

The enduring nature of this chivalrous element has been at-tested by Samuel P. Huntington's remark that the Americans characteristically must condemn war as being foreign to liberal goals, in terms of maximum freedom for the individual, or else see it "as an ideological movement in support of those goals."[21] In other words, they are incapable generally of seeing war as an instrument of national foreign policy in the same manner that Clausewitz did. Furthermore, in the field of literature the conception of war as romance did not end with the nineteenth century. V. S. Pritchett has observed that both Stephen Crane and Ernest Hemingway are capable of suggesting that they have actually been on the scene of a given battle but were not there out of necessity. Rather they were there as "daring, romantic, half-exalted, half-melancholy connoisseurs of courage and cowardice in a folly that could never be laid at their door."[22]

If in late nineteenth-century America war was not thought of as a primary means of regulating external questions, it was looked upon as a salutary exercise—a tonic against the materialism of modern life. From the security of the Washington of that day Henry Adams could write, "The few examples offered by history of great political societies, relieved from external competition or rivalry, were not commonly thought encouraging. War had been the severest test of political and social character, laying bare whatever was feeble, and calling out whatever was strong."[23] Theodore Roosevelt has been compared to Kaiser Wilhelm II in that he loved military power, discipline, and patriotism as abstract "good" things, not as the means to fight any particular war.[24] This attitude is reflected in a remark he made in 1890, well before his appointment as Assistant Secretary of the Navy: "It is not an economy—it is niggardly and foolish shortsightedness—to cramp our naval expenditures while squandering money right and left on everything else, from pensions to public buildings."[25] It was an attitude that was to dominate American thinking up to 1917. As late as 1913 Secretary of the Navy Daniels had sanguine hopes of "developing the Navy into a 'great university.' "[26] In 1915 Woodrow Wilson could still say that in the raising and arming of American forces there was "no threat lifted against any man, against any nation, against any interest but just a great solemn evidence that the force of America is the force of moral principle."[27]

Benedetto Croce has remarked that in Europe in the eighteenth century there arose a general impatience with "books stuffed with accounts of wars and of negotiations which prepared and ended them" and an increasing demand for histories of the arts, manners, morals, science and philosophy—i.e., of civilization.[28] The same tendency cropped up in America in the nineteenth century in the public lecture system in New England, in the Chautauqua Assembly, in the Thanatopsis Society of Gopher Prairie. This interest in civilization as opposed to war combined with native American idealism to give rise to the assumption underlying the two most important American war novels written in the nineteenth century—*Billy Budd* (c. 1888) and *The Red Badge of Courage* (1895). The assumption was that war was essentially an outdated institution and therefore one that could be treated objectively. Objectivity of treatment is the quality that distinguishes these two novels from all other war novels ever written in the United States; it places them in a special category which might be called that of the "pure" war novel—the work of fiction that treats some aspect of warfare coolly and dispassionately, having no basis in firsthand personal experience and believing that such experience is not likely to become available in the future.

Stephen Crane's novel stands suspended, as it were, in theme and style between the chivalrous memory of the War Between the States and the unforeseen reality of World War I. Henry Fleming is typical of "the young volunteers who poured out in their romantic thousands,"[29] bedazzled by dreams of glory and hoping that their mothers would sternly advise them to return bearing their shields or being borne on them. Crane's depiction of battle is also a forecast of the formless, incomprehensible, dehumanized slaughter that was to characterize the protest of the World War I novelists. The confusion felt by Fleming and his comrades in the retreats and countermarches and their indignation and fear at the sight of death wounds delivered by an unseen enemy foreshadow the trauma of the American soldier who found himself in the absurd charnel house of World War I.

On the other hand, the despair common to the post-World War I authors is nowhere evident in Crane's novel. In fact, Crane's treatment of his theme in *The Red Badge of Courage* is far more optimistic than in many of his other works such as *Maggie,* "The Blue Hotel," and "The Open Boat." His hero is set down in the context of battle, a context which forces him to face the primordial question of personal courage. The war is a closed system—a device that permits Crane to manipulate his protagonist, to observe his reactions, and to draw conclusions. Henry Fleming experiences fear, he runs away, he is ashamed, he returns to his comrades and fights bravely; in the end he marches away with them. The regiment is still intact; the bond of comradeship remains warm and reassuring, where in future American novels like John Dos Passos's *Three Soldiers* (1921) or Norman Mailer's *The Naked and the Dead* (1948) it was to be revealed as a bitter illusion. In the end Henry has proved himself; the sun breaks through the clouds. The reader is sure that the war will come to a logical conclusion in the sense that a clear-cut victory will emerge and that victory will actually further the ends of the victor. This was one of the assumptions about war that was to be most severely tested in the novels of a later era.

If Crane takes the Civil War (in fact a rather limited segment of it) to serve as the frame of reference in which his character moves, Herman Melville restricts his experiment even more severely. The dimensions of *Billy Budd* are of a classic starkness; the cramped quarters of a sailing ship suggest reassuringly that Billy's fate, although it may have a universal significance on another plane, falls within the realm of comprehension in terms of military justice. Like Crane, Melville could not foresee the impact that mechanized slaughter could have on war literature.[30] In his ironic poem "A Utilitarian View of the Monitor's Fight," he suggests that war has now become a business for mechanics: "War is now placed/ Where War belongs/Among the trades and artisans."[31] In other words, he was able to forecast that the age of mechanized warfare meant the end of the soldier's traditionally glamorous image, but he had no idea of the enormous slaughter this type of warfare would bring nor of the horrified reaction of writers like Hemingway and Cummings. In fact his attitude toward warfare rarely descends to the ironic level of "The Monitor's Fight." In most of his Civil War poems (e.g., "On Sherman's Men," "Inscription," "The Fortitude of the South," "Rebel Color-Bearers at Shiloh") he accepts the heroic view of combat. Hence Billy's fate is tragic but not absurd; as in all classic tragedy there is an element of reassurance, a suggestion that the life of the individual has a significant meaning and that to the dispassionate observer (in this case the American people) there is a valuable lesson to be learned.

Melville treats the theme of military discipline in purely idealistic terms. He himself had been outraged by the corporal punishment administered to the men on board the American man-of-war in which he hitched a ride home from the South Seas,[32] but here he presents his point of view on discipline much more subtly than he does in *White Jacket*. He complicates the problem both by making Captain Vere fair-minded, perspicacious, humane, and educated and by having Billy impressed; had Billy volunteered to serve under the Articles of War his punishment would have been an occupational hazard. For all the crude symbolism of Billy's farewell to the *Rights of Man* and the contrast between his angelic fairness of coloring and Claggart's blackness, the problem of his guilt or innocence is subtle and intricate. Furthermore, both Billy and Claggart may be given typically American symbolic values. Billy is simple, strong, and generous—a child of nature embodying the American dream of innocence like Pecos Bill, Johnny Appleseed, or Paul Bunyan; Claggart is the dark avatar of the Old World, the Royal Navy, and all that is glib and sophisticated. Characteristically Billy is inarticulate in a crisis and must resort to violence as an instinctive solution to problems too immediate or too deep for the frontier mentality. His trial and execution by the forces of enlightened society, embodied in Captain Vere, are at once a commentary on how discipline might be administered and an oblique suggestion that in the New World a new order of justice might be conceived that could transcend such harshness.

One can appreciate the academic quality of Crane's and Melville's treatment of the theme of war if one contrasts *Billy Budd* and *The Red Badge of Courage* with the stories of Ambrose Bierce. *Tales of Soldiers and Civilians* was written at about the same time as these works; but in tone, attitude, and appreciation of the true nature of warfare it was generations ahead of its time. Where one can observe certain links between *The Red Badge of Courage* and the novels that were to come out of World War I, one is struck by the manner in which Bierce's stories prefigure the novels of writers of the fifties like Norman Mailer and John Horne Burns. The desperate pessimism that tends to disfigure Bierce's work is perhaps paralleled in American letters only by that of James T. Farrell's Studs Lonigan series, but in the treatment of war itself Bierce adumbrated the attitudes of the generation that came to maturity in the shadow of nuclear warfare. Certain passages—like that in "An Affair of the Outposts" in which a civilian, caught in the midst of a battle, realizes that "it was an ugly and sickening business: to all that was artistic in his nature, revolting, brutal, in bad taste"[33]—suggest the tone of the novels of protest that were to come out of World War I. Even more striking are passages like that in "The Coup de Grace": "The enemy's fallen had to be content with counting. But of that they got enough: many of them were counted several times, and the total, as given afterward in the official report of the victorious commander, denoted rather a hope than a result,"[34] which could easily have been written about the war in Viet Nam. In other words, the American writer who had been in action adopted an attitude similar to that of subsequent generations who had shared his experience; Crane and Melville, writing at least one remove from the facts of war, tended to structure those facts in accordance with a national mythos.

The same idealism and theoretical approach that underlies *The Red Badge of Courage* and *Billy Budd,* coupled with naiveté and lack of experience rather than the pragmatism and delight in practical experimentation inherent in the American character, were among the factors that led the United States into World War I. The basis for American participation in that war was emotional rather than realistic—a culmination of a long series of factors, none of which was based on practical necessity.

In the late nineteenth century continued isolationism would have been the United States' wisest policy from a purely practical point of view. Before the Civil War there existed a certain element of interference in American affairs from Great Britain, which would like to have seen North America divided into a number of sovereign states that could be played off one against the other in order to maintain the primary influence of the British fleet in the Atlantic. However, the Civil War had the effect of unifying the nation against outside interference, and, with Canada serving as a hostage to ensure Britain's good behavior, the only serious foreign threat was nullified.[35]

Considering that neither Britain nor the United States herself officially sanctioned an expansionist policy, one can only conclude that American military growth and strategic involvement before World War I derived from origins that were psychological and theoretical. Imperialism was a commonly favored theme among political scientists, sociologists, and historians in late nineteenth-century America;[36] works such as Professor John W. Burgess's *Political Science and Comparative Constitutional Law* (1890) with its doctrine of "Nordic supremacy" and the British sociologist Benjamin Kidd's *Social Evolution* (published New York, 1894) argued that the more advanced nations must take charge of expansion and development of the tropics as world food requirements increased.

This variation on the theme of the white man's burden found a sympathetic echo in the thinking of Admiral Mahan, who said, "The 'mission' of Christian civilization 'which it must fulfil or perish,' was 'to overspread and assimilate to its own ideals those ancient and indifferent civilizations . . . at the head of which stand China, India and Japan.' "[37] Walter Millis has also remarked on the nonpractical element in American foreign policy: "It was the first battleship bill of 1890 which set the nation upon the alluring, the *somewhat metaphysical* and hitherto untrodden paths of 'sea power,' which were to invite us to assert an aggressive force upon world affairs."[38] S. P. Huntington has said that after 1870 the military, especially the army, campaigned with almost religious fervor (Huntington refers to them as regarding America from their "professional monastery") for greater recognition as a means of counteracting the materialistic decadence of civilian life.[39]

The importance of Admiral Mahan's *The Influence of Sea Power upon History* derives less from his strategic doctrines, most of which are specious, than from the manner in which he gave voice and form to a tendency that was ripening in the American spirit. He wrote the right book at the right time. On the political side President Harrison, Secretary of the Navy Tracy, and Congress (both houses of which were Republican) were interested in commercial expansion and in having a fleet. On the emotional side the nation was awakening to its own strength and beginning to flex its muscles. The roar of approval with which it greeted the caperings of Teddy Roosevelt and his Rough Riders was an expression of America's satisfaction at having at last engaged in and won an international competition.

In *War and Its Causes* Luther L. Bernard has argued that the United States participated in the Spanish-American War and in World War I under pressure from industrialists who had most to gain from extending their markets or who needed to protect loans made to the Allies in World War I.[40] These arguments, even though they may have carried considerable weight when the wars occurred, still ignore the powerful emotional pressures which also caused the nation to participate in these wars. Spain represented no real economic threat to the United States in the late nineteenth century, and the World War I loans were written off in the long run. The United States became involved in these wars because the means—the navy—existed; in turn, the navy's rise to eminence rested on subtle and intricate motivations that were neither economic nor entirely rational. As Richard Van Alstyne has observed, "Most persons [in America in 1914] . . . saw in the war no issue that would affect the United States in other than an emotional or sentimental way."[41] Furthermore, none of the reasons for which a country goes to war cited by Bernard (i.e., fear of aggression, financial and administrative imperialism, a need for expanding markets, a lack of raw materials, food, or living room)[42] applies to the situation in the United States before World War I.

The experience of war was to have a shattering effect on the American attitude toward warfare and the mood of the literature that came out of the war; but as the United States stood on the threshold of its first real battle, the concepts fundamental to *Billy Budd* and *The Red Badge of Courage* (i.e., that war was a phenomenon having a beginning, a middle, and an end; that war had a rational and attainable purpose; and that the individual, either as observer or participant, could benefit from the experience of war) were still intact.

THE AMERICAN SOLDIER IN FICTION, 1880–1963

PART ONE: 1917 – 1939

1. THE CRUSADE

In the very early days of World War I, an editorial writer in *The Nation* quoted Maurice Hewlett's suggestion that authors who take the war as their theme should "seek . . . simplicity, a quiet sensing of one or another aspect of human suffering, a not too vainglorious rendering of national aspiration, and, above all, a heart sensitive to 'the subdued wail of women and children,' a 'faculty of tears.' "[1] The early novels of the war tended to transgress or caricature these guidelines. The viewpoint was usually doctrinaire in that the tone and mood were pro-Entente and prowar; characters and situations were stereotypes based on patterns supplied by the melodramatic Entente propaganda. The "faculty of tears" was sentimental rather than humane, in keeping with a national literary taste that ran to *Pollyanna, Mrs. Wiggs,* and *The Winning of Barbara Worth.*

From the earliest days of the war, established writers like Temple Bailey and Mary Raymond Shipman Andrews rushed into print with patriotic potboilers like *Old Glory* (1917), *The Tin Soldier* (1918), and *Joy in the Morning* (1919)—all of which are more or less devoted to the theme of the war as a crusade against the Hun. Arthur Guy Empey actually joined the British Army, was wounded and invalided home, and made a successful lecture tour. His experiences formed the basis of his novel *Over the Top* (1917) which has a thirty-five-page glossary to explain the soldier slang. In *The Glory of the Trenches* (1918) Coningsby Dawson, like the lady authors, concentrates on the crusading aspect of the American effort. The patriotic enthusiasm of these early novelists was somewhat tempered by Edward Streeter's best-sellng *Dere Mable* (1918), a facetious series of letters from a country boy in the army to his sweetheart. Edith Wharton made her contribution to the literature of stereotype in *The Marne.*

The jingoistic attitudes of these writers was largely due to the fact that in matters of propaganda the English had several advantages over the Germans: there was the common bond of language with the United States, there was a long tradition of good relations between the British and American press corps, and the Americans were already in the habit of obtaining their European news via the British wire service.[2] They reinforced these advantages by having the Royal Navy haul the international telegraph cables out of the ocean and cut them, thereby effectively severing communications between Germany and America.[3] Under these circumstances the tales of German atrocities in France and Belgium went largely uncontested.

For the men who actually went overseas to fight, the propaganda hullabaloo produced in America by George Creel's Committee on Public Information eventually proved either embarrassing or repulsive. In *Personalities and Reminiscences of the War* Major General Robert L. Bullard, who had commanded an American Corps in France, says that while the military organization staggered under its new burdens of organization, training, and supply and accomplished little, the news media kept up a barrage of propaganda extolling the American effort, thereby causing ill-feeling among the troops and against the American forces by the French. "However good our intentions, what we were accomplishing at the scene of war was trifling, ridiculous, pitiful. . . . [The troops] were shamed to silence."[4] Intemperate and dishonest propaganda of this type underlies the scene from John Dos Passos's later novel *Three Soldiers,* where a dying soldier says,

"D'you know what I wish? I wish the war'd gone on and on until every one of them bastards had been killed in it."
"Which bastards?"
"The men who got us fellers over here."[5]

Despite the stereotyped aspects of these novels, Mrs. Wharton, like Willa Cather, wrote some of the more enduring works in the prowar category. The success of both these authors depends on their treatment of the effects of war on the personality of the individual rather than on their appreciation of the significance of the war. They both tend to see the war in rather simplified terms, as an event in which the forces of right are heavily concentrated on the Allied side. To them the war is ultimately a satisfying rather than a frustrating experience. Their protagonists meet death in the trenches but are satisfied to die in this manner, and it is implied that the war will ultimately achieve the objective of making the world safe for democracy. Claude Wheeler's death prevents him from having to experience the disillusionment of postwar life: "He died believing his country better than it is, and France better than any country can ever be."[6] Similarly, in *A Son at the Front* the death of George Campton comes to be accepted by his father as a beautiful and meaningful sacrifice. The elder Campton feels that great things have always come of human self-sacrifice, as he consoles himself with the thought that "the point was to remember that the efficacy of the sacrifice was always in proportion to the worth of the victim."[7]

Both of these writers emphasize the crusading element in the American war effort. In *One of Ours* there is a strong resemblance between Claude's going to war and Enid's going off to do missionary work in China; Enid goes away to save a sister, America's young men go away to save a sister nation. In the novels of both writers there is a rather stern Spartan attitude toward sending young men off to war. Claude Wheeler's mother says before he leaves for Europe, "When I was young, back in Vermont, I used to wish that I had lived in the old times when the world went ahead by leaps and bounds. And now, I feel as if my sight couldn't bear the glory that beats upon it."[8] The glory that beats upon her sight is the prospect of America delivering France from the Hun. America's youth is sent forth not merely to fight a war but to fulfill a sacred trust of heroic magnitude. Miss Cather deliberately evokes Odyssean images from time to time: "Like the hero of the Odyssey upon his homeward journey, Claude had often to tell what his country was, and who were the parents that begot him";[9] and "Youths were sailing away to die for an idea, a sentiment, for the mere sound of a phrase . . . and on their departure they were making vows to a bronze image in the sea."[10] In this way she implicitly equates the American war effort with the feats of the classic heroes or with the angels: "That was one of the things about this war; it took a little fellow from a little town, gave him an air and a swagger, a life like a movie film,—and then a death like the rebel angels."[11]

To this extent at least, then, Mrs. Wharton and Miss Cather aligned themselves with the older generation of established writers and scholars, those men who formed the backbone of the National Institute of Arts and Letters and who tended to be strongly in favor of war with Germany for the most jingoistic reasons. Charles A. Fenton has commented on the bloodthirstiness of this group, many of whom resigned from the Institute in protest over its support of neutrality, called for Theodore Roosevelt to return and lead the cause, and employed their vast influence in periodicals like *Life* to commit the nation to war: "[They] were hungry for drums and rhetoric rather than the harsh discipline of an exacting President."[12] Edith Wharton, in fact, said in November 1916, "The election [of Wilson] was a bitter humiliation to all of us Americans in France";[13] and Henry James, then resident in England, strongly supported a policy of intervention, finally becoming a British subject as a supreme gesture of support for the cause.

Still, in fairness one must note that a strong emotional bond existed between American intellectuals as a group and the Old World which symbolized the aesthetic values they sought after unsuccessfully in the New. There is the motif of the alienated American soldier who finds a kinship with the Europeans: Dos Passos's Andrews, Hemingway's Lieutenant Henry, Mrs. Wharton's George Campton, Miss Cather's Claude Wheeler, and Cummings himself all suggest that they are fighting not so much to defend American democracy as to protect a source of intellectual stimulation which they feel their country has failed to provide them. Andrews finds delight and intellectual fulfillment in the company of the Parisians; Henry's enjoyment of Italian culture and the Italian springtime is balanced by a Hemingwayesque satisfaction of the fleshly appetites. Europe existed as a cultural heritage for the more sensitive members of the American youth, and they were willing to make any sacrifice to protect it. Nothing could illustrate this more clearly than the fact that Cummings, who is usually cast as the arch-leader of the "disillusioned," enlisted in the United States Infantry only shortly after his release from the French prison of La Ferté. Only the termination of the war prevented his going into combat.[14]

For all the later vogue of disillusionment fostered by Cummings, Hemingway, and Dos Passos, the idealism and simplicity of spirit expressed in the works of Miss Cather and Mrs. Wharton represent accurately the mood of the young men who went away to war. The later reaction against warfare has tended to obscure the truth of Claude Wheeler's thought that "in this mass and movement of men there was nothing mean or common."[15] Fenton has questioned the extent to which the later authors' attitude of disillusionment was representative of those men who volunteered for service early in the war. In a study of the reminiscences of some hundreds of ambulance and camion drivers—most of whom were college educated—he found that the work was "unpleasant, exhausting, dangerous, requiring a high degree of individual initiative and responsibility"; i.e., it was not as detached as Malcolm Cowley later suggested. Most of these young men transferred to combat arms when the United States entered the war, and the vast majority of them "sustained throughout the war and into the peace a firm belief in the validity and necessity of their conduct."[16] Archibald MacLeish also commented on this point in a review of Laurence Stallings's *The First World War* (1939). He said that Stallings's book is not about World War I but about "World War II"—

the war as recreated by historians, political analysts, and economists: "Its actors are not men, nor even armies, but nations, continents. Its stories are . . . the greed of bankers, the treachery of politicians, the rapacity of munitions makers."[17]

Since 1918 so much has been written about the war that the atmosphere of the time has been destroyed, especially the real elements of sacrifice and courage of which the participants were consciously aware. Perhaps the most potent and the least tangible factor underlying American involvement in the war was the quality of native idealism, a quality that was a natural by-product of a simple and optimistic national outlook. Walter Millis has shown how the atrocity story was used to fill the void created when Allied newsmen were prevented from reporting the facts about Allied retreats in the early days of the war.[18] But these stories also served another function: they appealed directly to the emotions and ideals of American youths and helped convince them they were embarking on a great crusade. The balanced viewpoint must after all subscribe to Eugene Löhrke's comment: "That very remote literature of war idealism was often very pure. Its appeal, thin and fine as a bugle note, is not to be resisted."[19]

On the other hand, if *One of Ours* falls most clearly into the category of the prowar novel, Willa Cather also hints at least at the concept of war that came to characterize the work of the second-generation novelists of World War I. She implies the universality of modern war and the extent to which it reaches beyond the battlefield to touch the lives of everyone. She is perhaps the first American writer to recognize that the nature of war had altered dramatically in the twentieth century and that the rhetoric of war had acquired new meanings. In the matter of invasions, for example, she saw that the American presence in France was not greatly different from that of the Germans: "[It] was an invasion like the other. The first destroyed material possessions, and this threatened everybody's integrity."[20] Similarly, in describing the early news of the war she is able to relate the events in Europe to the fortunes of the people in America who still considerd themselves outside the scope of the conflict:

Even to these quiet wheat-growing people [of Nebraska] the siege guns before Liège were a menace; not to the safety of their goods, but to their comfortable, established way of thinking. They introduced the greater-than-man force which afterward repeatedly brought into this war the effect of unforeseeable natural disaster, like tidal waves, earthquakes, or the eruption of volcanoes. . . .

. . . the papers were full of accounts of the destruction of civilian populations. Something new, and certainly evil, was at work among mankind. Nobody was ready with a name for it. None of the well-worn words descriptive of human behaviour seemed adequate. The epithets grouped about the name of "Attila" were too personal, too dramatic, too full of old, familiar human passion.[21]

Her insight displayed in these passages is truly remarkable; it indicates that she was aware of an element which underlies the protest of the second-generation novelists and which in some cases they failed to formulate with anything like her clarity. *One of Ours* and *A Son at the Front* fall primarily into the category of prowar idealism, but they also look forward to the most typically American war novels—the literature of protest.

2. PROTEST

For a nation with an optimistic and rather idealistic outlook, World War I was calculated to provide the ultimate emotional shock. It illustrated both man's organizing ability and the limitations of his imagination; the same genius that could raise, train, equip, and transport practically the whole adult male population of two continents boggled at the problem of the machine gun. Inadequate development of the elements of armor and communications left the infantry aligned against machine guns and massed artillery, with the result that both sides suffered some of the most appalling losses in history. The bankruptcy of tactical doctrine at this point is illustrated by incidents like that in *The Enormous Room* where Cummings refers to the French machine gunners firing on their own infantry to force them to attack: "O we went forward. Yes. Vive le patriotisme";[1] and in Major General Bullard's assertion that the American military police had to form an unbroken line behind the infantry for the same purpose.[2] Eventually these tactics resulted in mutinies in the French and Russian armies in 1916 and 1917.

America sent a particularly sensitive group of men to experience the special horrors of the Great War. The volunteers who joined the ambulance and camion service must have been one of the most literate bodies of men ever assembled to do battle—men fresh from the universities, who had inherited a characteristic optimism and idealism and yet, insofar as they had been influenced by the muckraking tradition, were primed for protest. They suddenly found themselves in an absurd world, experiencing too much horror and able to see too little of the purpose of the operations in which they were engaged. Speaking of the memoirs produced by many European officers, Clennell Wilkinson has said, "In the trenches infantry officers led rather lonely, introspective lives. Every subaltern sat in judgment, not only upon the nations for going to war, but upon warfare itself. And he found it beastly."[3] For the American, lacking even the European's experience of previous wars, the effect was intensified. Out of this experience derived the element of protest in the works of the second-generation war novelists.

To writers like Laurence Stallings, William March, James

Stevens, and Thomas Boyd, the sheer scale of the slaughter ranked high as a subject of protest, as it did for Hemingway and Cummings who followed them. Even Edith Wharton and Willa Cather had been aware of this unfortunate aspect of the war. Claude Wheeler and Sergeant Hicks are astonished at the young British soldier who tells them that his battalion went into an attack a thousand strong and came back seventeen, but the fictional account is no exaggeration of what really happened.[4] Although the American dead from wounds and disease amounted to only two percent of the troops engaged compared to nearly twenty-five percent for other nationalities,[5] the Americans were in action for only slightly over a year. Thus their losses were still alarmingly high and gave rise to the outlook described by Hemingway in *A Farewell to Arms* (1929): "I had seen nothing sacred, and the things that were glorious had no glory and sacrifice was like the stockyards at Chicago if nothing [was] done with the meat except bury it."[6]

Even given a slaughter on a completely unforeseen scale and the sort of heartless incompetence on the part of the officers mentioned by Hemingway and Cummings, the war might still have been a great deal less shocking if it had not been for the element of accidental, meaningless, purely gratuitous death. Both large-scale operations and sheer stupidity are capable of being recognized as the product of the human mind and therefore of finding some sort of reconciliation with those persons who are exposed to them, but it was the aspect of the war as a mindless destroyer of human dignity that proved to be the most debilitating, as Edith Wharton was the first to note: "Some of these histories . . . were abominable, unendurable, in their long-drawn useless horror."[7] In Boyd's *Through the Wheat* (1923), the protagonist Private Hicks is brave enough, not particularly idealistic, even slightly cynical about the war and its results; but the sense of futility and his reaction against fighting are brought to a head when he sees a heavy branch, previously partly severed by a shell, fall out of a tree and kill a sleeping soldier. Hicks is not really afraid of death, " 'But the war seems so damned ridiculous. Take our going over the other day. A full battalion starting off and not even a fifth of them coming back. And what did they do? We never even saw a German. They just laid up there and picked us off—direct hits with their artillery every time! That's hell, . . . you know.' "[8]

Even as poor a stick as Parve Mattock, sycophant and informer, comes to feel vitiated by the war and the injustices he has seen: "It seemed like the war had used up everything I had when I came into the army; and all that I had left was simply rotten, and that was all there was to it."[9] The death's head that grins from beneath Cumming's near-hysterical humor is another manifestation of the sense of absurdity induced by the war as he saw it: "Maybe someday we'll all of us go skating on the canals; and maybe we'll talk about what happens when the dikes break, and about the houses and the flowers and the windmills."[10] Hemingway might have been speaking for the whole generation of war novelists when he summed up the experience of the war in the passage in which Major Rinaldi questions Henry about the circumstances surrounding his wound: " 'They say if you can prove you did any heroic act you can get the silver. Otherwise it will be the bronze. Tell me exactly what happened. Did you do any heroic act?' 'No,' I said. 'I was blown up while were were eating cheese.' "[11] What he is expressing is the realization that in a war of this type and magnitude, bravery did not matter, professional competence did not matter, devotion and self-sacrifice did not matter. Accidental and pointless death had become commonplace: " 'I was blown up while we were eating cheese.' "

Furthermore, the conflict introduced perhaps the most demoralizing aspect of modern war: the dehumanization of combat. The entire process, from recruiting to the engagement of the enemy, seemed to be the operation of a machine rather than the result of human volition. Dos Passos invokes the image of the production line in the chapter headings of *Three Soldiers*: "Making the Mould," "The Metal Cools," "Machines," "Rust," "The World Outside," and "Under the Wheels." Everywhere there is the suggestion that the war is a self-generating force and that a given operation, once begun, must run its course. As the French general says when an aviator comes to warn him that his guns are firing on his own troops, " 'On a commencé, il faut finir.' "[12]

The sensation of being trapped by a huge and ruthless machine was particularly horrifying to a generation that went to war as they might have gone to a picnic. An element that strongly unifies all the novels of World War I and differentiates them as a group from those written about World War II is that in the former the soldiers tend to want to get into action for its own sake; they look on the war as an adventure they do not want to miss. In the latter the soldiers want to get into action only as a means of accomplishing an unpleasant task which will allow them to return home as quickly as possible. Not all the characters in the World War I novels are as idealistically motivated as Troy Belknap in *The Marne* or George Campton in *A Son at the Front*, both of whom wish to serve the idea of France as an abstract good. Claude Wheeler in *One of Ours* and Cummings share this motivation to a certain extent, just as Hemingway does about Italy. But Claude also goes to war in order to escape the stifling intellectual atmosphere of a small midwestern town and to find both the physical and spiritual adventure so notably lacking in America. The war is a picnic or a Boy Scout outing to the splendid chaps from America. No oath or blasphemy passes their lips as they swing toward the front: " 'Well, we can't arrive any too soon for us, boys?' The sergeant looked over his shoulder and they grinned, their teeth showing white in their red, perspiring faces."[13] And when they are arrived in the trenches, Claude reckoned "now that he was here, he would enjoy the scenery a bit." He stands up on the firing step and admires the dawn, a little disappointed that nothing is happening. In fact, the war often proved less stimulating than these young men had hoped; the sense of adventure, like the recurring desire to be a pure and romantic hero, was smothered by the monotonous army existence.

The very brevity of America's participation in the war produced a sense of frustration. The Americans were in the war in time to experience the depression of its darkest hour—the collapse of Russia, the mutinies in XVI French Army Corps, and the last great German offensive—without actually enjoying the sensation of a clear-cut victory which would have alleviated this experience. The lateness of their arrival on the scene gave rise to the bitter crack among some of the Allies about the Rainbow Division: "They came after the storm." Dixon Wecter has said, "The end was abrupt. It left us with tense nerves and unspent effort. A cheap victory was almost an immoral one."[14] In addition the United States lost its invaluable prestige as a major neutral power by entering the war and gained nothing in return. All in all the nation, like many of the individuals who went overseas, paid a high price in frustration and disillusionment for an involvement that had been largely altruistic in its nature.

The usual responses to the trauma of the war and the sudden armistice are those in which the individual either makes a private peace or else is permanently alienated from society by the enormity of what he has experienced. John Andrews, Frederick Henry, Nick Adams, and to a certain extent Cummings try to make a separate peace, usually with unhappy results. The attempt to withdraw from an experience that is chaotic and absurd is rationalized in various ways, although at bottom it derives from an inability to comprehend the meaning of the war. Lieutenant Henry's armistice, for example, is in no way inspired by the mood of "Andiamo a casa" of the Italian soldiers. On one level it is a preservation of selfhood in the midst of chaos:

You saw emptily, lying on your stomach, having been present when one army moved back and another came forward. You had lost your cars and your men as a floorwalker loses the stock of his department in a fire. There was, however, no insurance. You were out of it now. You had no more obligations. If they shot floorwalkers after a fire in the department store because they spoke with an accent they had always had, then certainly the floorwalkers would not be expected to return when the store opened again for business. They might seek other employment; if there was any other employment and the police did not get them.[15]

On another level it is plain desertion. Similarly John Andrews in *Three Soldiers* sees his desertion and subsequent surrender to the authorities as a meaningful act, a restatement of his significance as an individual; but in the light of his ineffective conduct while he is free it is hard to give very much weight to this interpretation of his action. Much more acceptable is the private peace of Nick Adams who volunteered, served bravely, was smashed by impersonal forces, and saw no point in throwing away what life remained for the sake of an abstract idea:

Nick sat against the wall of the church where they had dragged him to be clear of the machine gun fire in the street. Both legs stuck out awkwardly. He had been hit in the spine. . . . Nick turned his head and looked down at Rinaldi. "Senta Rinaldo; Senta. You and me we've made a separate peace." Rinaldi lay in the sun, breathing with difficulty. "We're not patriots."[16]

Later, in *For Whom the Bell Tolls*, the value of an individual gesture was to be emphasized as opposed to the idea of a private armistice, but in the novels about World War I Hemingway and his confreres saw the private armistice as one acceptable mode of action in a situation that seemed to be larger than the human mind could grasp. It is an important reaction, and one that links many of the American war novels, but at this stage it was still an embryonic response in that the individual usually made his private armistice with the object of saving his own skin. Some years later when the private peace was to reappear in the American war novel, it acquired a new and larger significance.

William L. Stidger—a Methodist minister, YMCA secretary in France, and author of *Soldier Silhouettes*—saw battle as a spiritual purge. "No boy goes through the hell of fire and suffering and wounds that he does not come out new born. . . . The old man is gone from him and a new man is born in him."[17] There was an ironic truth to the minister's words, manifested in the recurrent motif of alienation by those men who had experienced the worst aspects of the war. In some cases, like that of Lieutenant Henry, the alienation takes the form of a nausea induced by the use of idealistic words and expressions: "Abstract words such as glory, honor, courage, or hallow were obscene."[18] More frequently one encounters men whose attempt to comprehend what they have seen has reoriented their scale of values and their perception of the world. When the elder Campton visited his wounded son he remarked on the difference "in him—in life—in everything."[19] Later, while George Campton was convalescing in Paris before returning to his regiment, "he gave the impression of having travelled far beyond such matters, and of living his life in some inconceivable region from which, with that new smile of his, he continued to look down unseeingly on his parents. 'It's exactly as if he were dead,' the father thought."[20]

The condition of Hicks in *Through the Wheat* is very similar. After incessant attacks and retreats, constant fighting, drilling, and seeing men killed, "Hicks tramped on through the field, dimly sensing the dead, the odors, the scene. . . . No longer did anything matter, neither the bayonets, the bullets, the barbed wire, the dead, nor the living. The soul of Hicks was numb."[21] And Mahon in Faulkner's *Soldiers' Pay* (1926), like Lazarus after his resurrection, existed in a dreaming, indifferent state not entirely due to his physical wound. For all these authors the Lazarus motif seems to symbolize the state of mind resulting from an attempt to comprehend the war. It suggests a great deal more than the trauma of American idealism in the face of the horrors of war; the effort involved in trying to understand the war moves the individual to a new plane of comprehension, but in the process it destroys him as a member of society.

In the circumstances it is the tough-minded individual who manages to survive the effects of the war. In *Soldiers' Pay* it is Private Gilligan and Sergeant Madden—both of whom are less susceptible to the vicissitudes of fate than either the officers or the raw conscripts—who survive and endure, but they do so at the cost of any ideals they might once have held. Both Lieutenant Henry and Cummings move from an enjoyment of the war as intellectual and aesthetic stimulus to a rejection of it as a soul-shattering absurdity beyond the comprehension or control of the human intellect, but in many cases the protagonists in the World War I novels begin and end their participation in the war on a purely selfish plane. Dick Savage, for example, in Dos Passos's *1919* (1932) devotes himself solely to self-gratification throughout his entire period of service. Private Parve Mattock goes to war for ill-defined and largely selfish reasons, never sees action, and passes his time trying to worm his way into the confidence of his superiors. He ends the war as a corporal, a reward for having acted as an informer reporting "Bolshevism" among his comrades to the Company Intelligence Officer. Finally there is the example of Krebs in Hemingway's *In Our Time* who went away to war with much the same motivation as Dick Savage or Private Fuselli, experienced a great deal of action, spent time in the army of occupation, and was in no particular hurry to return to civilian life. The cynical outlook necessary for survival in wartime makes civilian life an absurdity. In a way this suggests that the authors themselves were not fully able to understand the events of the war: Richard Savage is absorbed by those events; John Andrews attempts to make an act of rejection; Hemingway in his later works turned away from the limitless violence of the war toward the ritualized and comprehensible violence of the bullring; Cummings's laughter, while it suggested the manner in which novelists would eventually come to cope with the theme of warfare, was partially invalidated by his own reenlistment. In fact this task—the necessity to comprehend the nature of industrialized war and to show how the individual could act effectively in the face of that phenomenon— was not accomplished for another two generations. The authors who wrote about World War II largely ignored it and left it for the writers of the late fifties to deal with.

In America the Great War provided a curious combination of circumstances in that a particularly voluble group of young men went to Europe and were allowed to observe the war from what Malcolm Cowley has called a spectatorial point of view.[22] If these men were horrified by their experience of the war, they were also frustrated by its inconclusiveness. Most important, a greater proportion of them lived to tell about their experiences than was the case among the soldiers of the European armies. As a result the literature of protest in the United States parallels in quantity and quality that of the nations involved in the war for much longer periods. The works of these novelists represented the war as it really was; like the war itself they were realistic and horrifying, but they tended to fade with the passage of time. The works of Stallings, March, Stevens, and Boyd are still readable today but have the dated quality of a regimental reunion. The most enduring novels are those of Cummings, Hemingway, Dos Passos, and Faulkner in which the authors went beyond realism to take the war as a metaphor for the ills besetting their generation.

3. THE WAR AS METAPHOR

After the first spate of reminiscences and protest, war literature in Europe fell into limbo for a period of about ten years. Works like Henri Barbusse's *Under Fire (Le feu,* 1917) and Ernst Juenger's *Storm of Steel (Im Stahlgewittern,* 1920) were not followed by more enduring books about the war such as Robert Graves's *Goodbye to All That* until 1929. Arnold Zweig's *The Case of Sergeant Grischa (Der Streit um den Sergeanten Grischa),* one of the best war novels ever written, appeared in 1927; the most famous of all, Erich Maria Remarque's *All Quiet on the Western Front (Im Westen nichts Neues)* was published in 1929. In part this phenomenon may be attributed simply to war weariness in a continent tired of conflict; in part it was due to the serious economic and political problems which distracted Europe early in the twenties. Yet Eugene Löhrke has claimed that there were subtler reasons for the decline and resurgence of interest in war literature. Just as "men [had] wanted this . . . terrible release from the penalties of safety and monotony"[1] in 1914, now that the memory of its horrors had grown dim, they were glad enough to integrate its experiences into the nations' literatures. What Bernard Bergonzi calls the process of "remythologizing" the war began in Europe after approximately ten years of convalescence.

The conversion of the war into literary capital also took place in America, but it began much sooner than in Europe. The popular taste for war literature fell off sharply in 1921 and did not completely reappear until the publication of *All Quiet on the Western Front.*[2] During this interval there was a tremendous vogue of works dealing with the evolution of civilization: Shaw's *Back to Methuselah,* Mumford's *Story of the Utopias,* Wells's and Van Loon's "outlines" of history, Frazer's *Golden Bough* all suggested to a disoriented nation that there was an element of continuity and progress in human affairs. Letters, reminiscences, and biographies of the leisurely Edwardian era were also popular; for other readers the literature of escape, especially to the South Seas, helped salve the memory of the war.[3] Nonetheless, the major American contributions to the literature of the Great War were written, if not necessarily acclaimed by the public, considerably before their

European counterparts. The Americans had been in action for only slightly more than a year; they had no problems of reconstruction to distract them; no Marshall Plan aid program involved them in Europe. The less shattering exposure to the war in economic terms and the abrupt ending allowed them to turn somewhat sooner to an artistic transmutation of what they had experienced. First on the scene was Dos Passos with *Three Soldiers* in 1921, followed by Cummings's *Enormous Room* in 1922. Faulkner published *Soldiers' Pay* in 1926, and *A Farewell to Arms*—the last major American novel of the Great War—appeared in 1929.

These four novelists—Hemingway, Dos Passos, Cummings, and Faulkner—are the "spectators" of whom Cowley speaks in *Exile's Return,* the men of whom it was said "If the war taught them bitterness, it was a bitterness tinged with longing and detached regret, a romantic distillation of other men's despair."[4] None of them served in a fighting arm; while their work shares the same note of protest as the novels of Stallings, Boyd, Stevens, and March, the real significance of their work lies elsewhere. It has been suggested that this generation's disillusion arose from "Versailles, Red scares, Harding normalcy and the gross materialism [of the twenties] rather than the war."[5] Vernon Parrington observed: "With the cynicism that came with post-war days the democratic liberalism of 1917 was thrown away like an empty whiskey-flask. Clever young men [said] that the first want of every man . . . is his dinner, and the second is his girl."[6] The shock effect of the war on American idealism and optimism was even reflected in contemporary typography; in the new consciousness of the insignificance of human action, "the letter 'i' often became lower case as the point of view of the narrator was lost in the general reductive terror."[7] In these circumstances the war provided a powerful metaphor, not only to express the reaction against postwar conditions but also to embody the spirit of the "lost generation." Observing that none of the postwar novelists presents a picture of settled and secure domestic life, Joseph Warren Beach remarks, "By one consent they have taken for their subject that unsettlement and instability which we must acknowledge to be a characteristic feature of our life both material and moral."[8] The retreat from Caporetto and the subsequent events of *A Farewell to Arms* thus become symbolic of the outlook of the twenties: the collapse of the Italian forces resembles the collapse of the moral certitude with which America entered the war; the chaos of the retreat itself parallels America's frenetic search for new values in the twenties; and Lieutenant Henry's desertion and subsequent tragic loss of his wife and child symbolize the sense of isolation expressed by many writers of this generation.

The tendency for the nobility of human conduct to be lost in an increasingly bureaucratic world is another one of the themes on which these novelists concentrate. Dos Passos's revolt "against the enslaving of minds and bodies that war entails"[9] deals especially with the problem of the artist trapped in the supreme bureaucracy of army life. Even though the war is over, the niggling regulations and the brutality of small men safely ensconced in a hierarchy manage to destroy John Andrews's attempts at artistic creation. For Cummings the war symbolized the destruction of the humanist by the bureaucracy. Alfred Kazin has noted that imprisonment in La Ferté gave Cummings a perspective on the war. For him "the enormous room concentrated the war."[10] The perspective that the room provided was a parody of the real war in the sense that the inmates, the jailers, and the physical conditions parodied the conduct of the statesmen and the conditions in the trenches. Cummings himself substantiates this point when he says, "[In watching the degradation of the prisoners of Macé] I realized fully and irrevocably and perhaps for the first time the meaning of civilization."[11] For Hemingway the war revealed that the soldier's bravery and competence were as nothing in front of the bureaucratic mind. Intelligence and common sense might urge the soldier to retreat, but if he did so the firing squad of the rear-echelon martinets threatened him with the ultimate disgrace.

The events of the war also provided an adequate symbol of the selfishness of society. Alan Calmer claims that the war aroused in Dos Passos "a sense of social injustice which became the guiding influence of his work."[12] This sense of social injustice is the basis of the blistering attack in *1919* and *Three Soldiers* on the officers, public relations personnel, YMCA secretaries, and socialites who made a career out of the war. The success of these people was in bitter contrast to the shattered lives of the masses of ordinary men. Like Henri Barbusse, Dos Passos focuses on the agony of the common people, but in the *U.S.A.* trilogy he goes beyond Barbusse to make the events of the war significant of the attitudes of an era. Cummings too reacts against the tendency to inundate the common man, with his references to "Les poilus divins," his delight in the "Delectable Mountains," and his farewell to Jean Le Nègre:

—Boy, Kid, Nigger with the strutting muscles—take me up into your mind once or twice before I die. . . . Quickly take me up into the bright child of your mind. . . . Take me up (carefully; as if I were a toy) and play carefully with me, once or twice, before I and you go into great Jack roses and ivory—(once or twice Boy before we together go wonderfully down into the Big Dirt laughing, bumped with the last darkness).[13]

Edmund Wilson said that "the barbarity of the world since the war" was the theme of *The Sun Also Rises*, just as it had been the theme of Hemingway's earlier work.[14] For William Faulkner, too, the war could be used to illustrate the ruthlessness with which society betrays its weaker members. For both of these writers the element of barbarity manifested itself most clearly in the relationships between men and women. In the novels of World War I, this relationship was usually tinged with the harsh caste of puritanism. Before having been in action at least, some young men like Fuselli, Mattock, and Cadet Lowe vaguely equated the possibility of romantic love with heroism on the battlefield—of modern-day knight errantry; but there was also an instinctive indictment of what the Americans regarded as European looseness or immorality in the domain of love. As they look at some French architecture, Fuselli and a companion seek to put their disapproval into words: " 'They didn't mind having naked women about did they?' . . . 'I bet they was immoral, them guys.' "[15] Another soldier expresses their common fear and resentment of the obviously experienced French women when he encounters one of them in a cafe: " 'Guess she thinks she's the Queen of the May.' . . . He turned to the woman and shouted in a voice full of hatred, 'Bon swar!' "[16] Claude Wheeler's priggery at the idea that a French woman had given birth to the child of a German soldier is paralleled by the essential puritanism of Lieutenant Henry's character in *A Farewell to Arms*. Teasing Henry in the mess, Major Rinaldi says, " 'I know you are the fine good Anglo-Saxon boy. I know. You are the remorse boy, I know. I will wait till I see the Anglo-Saxon brushing away harlotry with a toothbrush.' "[17]

In some cases—notably those of George Campton in *A Son at the Front,* Claude Wheeler in *One of Ours,* and Margaret Powers in *Soldiers' Pay*—combat provides a welcome alternative to a relationship that had become either too complex or too sterile to bear. The complexity especially of the full-blown love relationship was something the American was not prepared to cope with; to him it remained both literally and figuratively foreign. On the other hand, on those occasions when the sensitive American is stimulated by a different attitude toward love (as in the case of John Andrews who is moved to write a concerto entitled "La Reine de Saba"), this stimulation tends to set him in opposition to American mores. It could be argued that this incompatibility is one of the fundamental themes of that finest of American novels, *The Great Gatsby.* Here, as in *The Sun Also Rises,* the sharply etched images of sterility are reminiscent of those in Amy Lowell's "Patterns" and T. S. Eliot's "Waste Land" and thereby suggest the influence of the 1912 intellectual generation on the younger authors of the war. What Gatsby offers Daisy in his romantic wooing is too complicated and too much at variance with her social background for her to be able to comprehend or accept. Gatsby is unique in that he seeks the involvement of a love affair; most often the American soldier is shown as having been alienated from such a link with society by his experience of the war. The attitude of the majority of the fictional heroes who had been to war is summed up in an equivocal passage from *Soldiers' Pay*. Speaking of the transparency of Cecily's dress, Gilligan says, " 'Say, . . . you can see right through her.' 'Dat's de war,' explained the Negro driver, sleeping again immediately."[18]

Perhaps the most complete use of the war as metaphor occurs in Hemingway's *In Our Time*. The limitless violence of the war counterpoints the routine violence of the peacetime world; the mules drowning with their legs broken reproduce the agony of the grasshopper impaled on a fishhook; the fisherman's thoughtless cruelty is only a microcosm of the larger barbarity of mankind. In order to emphasize the absurdity of war in *A Farewell to Arms*, Hemingway refused Lieutenant Henry the gallantry of conduct he himself had displayed in similar circumstances. *In Our Time* employs the same technique of paring away life's compensations in order to leave a bleak portrait of existence. As Wilson has said, "The most remarkable effects of this fiction . . . are those . . . by which we are made to feel, behind the appetite for the physical world, the tragedy or the falsity of the moral relation."[19] The American soldiers generally, in the novels that came out of World War I, are characterized by an "appetite for the physical world" even more strongly marked than that of the soldiers in European fiction. Perhaps it is for this reason that the most enduring novels of the war use the war itself to symbolize the nation's spiritual malaise.

4. EUROPEAN CONTEMPORARIES

It is interesting to note the difference between the European attitude toward war and that of the Americans, mainly because such a contrast helps illustrate the nature of the American reaction to the war. The Americans experienced the same horrors as the Europeans; neither were equipped to understand the phenomenon of modern war or to think of it in other than misleading and outworn terminology. The greater degree of innocence and idealism of the Americans was perhaps counterbalanced by the longer period of exposure suffered by the Europeans. Yet one feels that the Europeans managed to avoid the depth of shock experienced by the Americans by developing a protective psychology which the Americans seemed unable to foster. In *A Son at the Front* Edith Wharton observed, "A nation in arms does not judge a war as simply as an army of professional soldiers,"[1] but it was exactly this professional simplicity of outlook which helped the Europeans endure the horrors they had to face. In *Goodbye to All That,* for example, Robert Graves says, "The battalion cared as little about the successes or reverses of our Allies as about the origins of the war. It never allowed itself to have any political feelings about the Germans. A professional soldier's duty was simply to fight whomever the King ordered him to fight."[2] Nowhere in American literature about World War I does one find the sort of flippant gaiety concealing real professional military competence that one sees in *Goodbye to All That.* Talking about a night patrol he led, Graves says, "We had got halfway back to our own trenches, when a German machine gun opened traversing fire along the top of our trenches. We immediately jumped to our feet; the bullets were brushing the grass, so to stand up was safer. We walked the rest of the way home."[3]

The point is that it really was safer to "walk the rest of the way home," but Graves makes it sound like an evening stroll. His book is actually a compendium of the lore of trench warfare written in a bantering tone; it illustrates how professional soldiers can impose form on what is essentially formless and chaotic, but in order to do so they must leave aside considerations of why they are fighting.

The suggestion that the war was stimulating and a valuable experience is not entirely restricted to men like Graves's professionals. Charles Edmonds, who served as a subaltern with the Royal Warwickshire Regiment, says that "he enjoyed being a soldier on the whole";[4] and Ernst Juenger found the war "manly and purposeful."[5] This attitude underlies an interesting element that sets European war literature apart from American: the relative dearth of escaping stories in the latter is in sharp contrast to the situation in European literature. In a review of the literature of the Great War, Clennell Wilkinson remarked, "It was noticeable . . . that in spite of the alleged disgust with the whole subject [of war] . . . the admirable series of books . . . describing semi-humorously the adventures of officers who escaped from prisons—continued to appear and to command large sales."[6] The same phenomenon was to appear in World War II; escaping stories formed a major category of European war literature but were almost nonexistent in America. This suggests the reaction of a society that accepts war as an integral and familiar factor in human affairs: to the Europeans, escaping is part of a rather exciting game in which both sides know the rules.

The Europeans, in other words, comprehended war and accepted it as a part of life. To the European the soldier is part of the social structure; in America he is an outsider. Thus General von Lychow, a humane and intelligent man, can delight in Sergeant Grischa as an instrument of battle: "Here stood the true fighting man, a good six feet of him, broad shoulders and sinewy chest designed and made for war, arms to strike with, legs to carry him to the attack";[7] and Grischa himself, the most peaceful of men, is proud of his skill and courage as a soldier. In 1917 the American General Bullard, living in a French mess where "the memory of no one of them could reach back for even a few weeks without coming upon comrades, brothers fallen and lost, gone as they must expect to go," was struck by the "quiet patience that amounted almost to cheerfulness";[8] war was part of life and had to be endured. Unfortunately this tradition of regimentation helped keep even the most sensitive Europeans moving steadily forward into the holocaust. Paul Bäumer, in *All Quiet on the Western Front*, is fully aware of his generation's alienation from German society as a result of the war. He muses sadly on the fact that he and his comrades, originally like coins from the currencies of the various German provinces, have been struck anew by the fiery imprint of war and can never again return into circulation; although he questions the system that produced these events, it never occurs to him or his comrades to make the gesture of protest so characteristic of the Americans like John Andrews, Frederick Henry, or Cummings.

It is exactly this note of personal outrage at the indignities of war and the militarist system—the tone of individual reaction— which provides the distinctive cachet of the American war novels. The Americans were steeped in whys and wherefores; they had a built-in emotional baggage which rendered them immediately vulnerable to the horror of what they were involved in and to subsequent questionings of abstract considerations such as the "success" or "failure" of their mission—a tendency which caused Malcolm Cowley, in a review of *1919*, to describe Dos Passos as "an aesthete moving about the world in a portable ivory tower."[9] John Andrews in *Three Soldiers* illustrates the enervating tendency of the Americans to think too precisely on the event in contrast with what appears to be European heartlessness. While he and a friend are in a railway waiting room trying to decide whether to go to Paris, a bottle of wine is broken, and a ragged dirty poilu standing nearby offers to eat the bottle for twenty centimes: "The man's teeth flashed and crunched down on the jagged edge of the glass. There was a terrific crackling noise. He flourished the bottle-end again. 'My God, he's eating it,' cried Henslowe, roaring with laughter, 'and you're afraid to go to Paris.' "[10] To the Europeans, although the scale of the war was unprecedentedly large, the experience of war was nothing new. It was another in a series of wars. Hence the European emphasis, in the accounts of the war, on the scope of the operations and the size of the casualty lists rather than on the element of emotional shock.

Perhaps the contrast between the European and the American war novel is most clearly indicated in two of the last novels written about the Great War: David Jones's *In Parenthesis* (1937) and Dalton Trumbo's *Johnny Got His Gun* (1939). The former is the culmination of the "remythologizing" process in which the vast experience of the war is assimilated into what is fundamentally a tribal consciousness. The events of the war, seen through the eyes of the Welsh privates, are related parenthetically to a body of national myth. Furthermore, the fact of being a soldier and the relationships induced by the war are understood instinctively, if not consciously, by these simple men. It never occurs to them to wonder about their relationship to each other and, most important, to the battalion officers. The battalion or the regiment, after all, retained a set of social characteristics which had been familiar to them all their lives: the officers were often drawn either from the gentry or the aristocracy, senior noncommissioned officers might well have held comparably responsible positions in civilian life, and the ordinary soldiers came mostly from the laboring classes. Also the regiment would often be named for the shire or county from which it was recruited. Thus *In Parenthesis*, like *The Case of Sergeant Grischa,* evokes "the spirit of kinship with all and partisanship with none."[11] This subtle quality of mutual affection and understanding parallels that surprising passage in Edmund Blunden's *Undertones of War* where Colonel Harrison of the 11th Royal Sussex Regiment, portrayed elsewhere as stern and aloof, watches the battalion go forward to one of the dreadful attacks on the Somme: "I watched [the Colonel] as he stood on the mound roof of his dugout, that simple and martial figure, calling out to those as they went in terms of faith and love."[12] The same spirit underlies Charles Edmonds's comment on two of the best-known English writers of the war, Siegfried Sassoon and Robert Graves: "Sassoon, like his friend Graves who served in the same regiment, was an exceptionally brave man and no defeatist. Both of them saw the War through, and reserved their comment, the sustaining factor for both of them being esprit-de-corps, a passionate addiction to their regiment and to their comrades whom they would not fail."[13] In all these works there exist the typically European sense of the regiment as a parochial entity and the events of the war as part of the mythos of the race.

By contrast, *Johnny Got His Gun* is war literature resulting from a purely rational rather than an instinctive or emotional process. Like John Hersey's *The War Lover* (1960), it is the expansion of a theme to its ultimate conclusion. Its protagonist is mutilated not merely in one of the various horrifying ways described in previous war novels; he is mutilated in all of them. He is the ultimate basket case, incapable of seeing or speaking but able to live and to think When he finally discovers a means of communicating with the nurses and doctors attending him, he asks that they either kill him or put him on display in a freak show as a warning to those martial spirits who would like to go to war again. His request is refused of course; killing him is against the rules, and the freak show would be bad publicity for the government. Trumbo's novel dwells on an absolute protest against war and, like so many American novelists, on the loneliness and isolation of the individual. For the American, war is not part of the order of things; no good can come of it, not even poetry.

5. THE THIRTIES

The decade of the thirties was marked by the return of the United States to a characteristic set of policies and attitudes after its unwonted excursion into foreign intervention during the war. In the field of foreign policy, independence of action, the essential element in American diplomacy before 1938, reasserted itself in the rejection of the Treaty of Versailles—a rejection which underlined the fact that the American people had not grasped the complexity and continuing menace of the world situation. The signing of the Kellogg-Briand Treaty "to renounce war as an instrument of national policy" and "to solve all disputes or conflicts of whatever origin by pacific means" reinforced the false American sense of security and undermined the position of the military establishment.[1] American idealism reemerged shortly thereafter in events such as the enunciation of the Hoover-Stimson doctrine of nonrecognition; the attempt to contain Japanese expansion in Manchuria by moral reprobation is strongly reminiscent of President Wilson's policy toward Germany in 1914 and had approximately the same effect.

By a curious paradox, the beginning of the Great Depression was accompanied by a resurgence of optimism on a national scale among many writers. Bernard De Voto claimed that the intellectual anarchy and despair of some writers between the wars not only did not reflect the national outlook but was the complete opposite of the truth; i.e., there was no correlation between literary *Weltschmerz* and national sentiment.[2] Malcolm Cowley observed that the postwar writers "were often described as being 'disillusioned,' but I have always felt that the adjective was badly chosen. They were something quite different: rebels in life and art. To be a rebel implies faith in one's ability to do things better than those in power."[3] To be sure, the end of the decade of the twenties marked the advent of a serious new challenge to the nation's writers. Mark Van Doren said, "When [Fitzgerald's] generation came to the sterner time after 1929 it had to give up its habits or else seem like an elderly beau, amusing to the youngsters."[4] Many of these writers have attested the new sense of purpose and challenge which accompanied the times. Phillip Rahv said, "In the early thirties we lived through a moment of high confidence and inspiration, a moment perhaps never to be recovered in our lifetime";[5] and Edmund Wilson, speaking of the period after the stock market crash, commented,

As conditions grew worse and worse and President Hoover, unable to grasp what had happened, made no effort to deal with the breakdown, a darkness seemed to descend. Yet, to the writers and artists of my generation who had grown up in the Big Business era and had always resented its barbarism, its crowding out of everything they had cared about, these years were not depressing but stimulating. One couldn't help being exhilarated at the sudden unexpected collapse of that stupid gigantic fraud. It gave us a new sense of freedom; and it gave us a new sense of power to find ourselves still carrying on while the bankers, for a change, were taking a beating.[6]

The experience of the war, the subsequent spectacle of the nations scrabbling for their own welfare at Versailles, and the crudeness and selfishness of the Harding-Coolidge era were frightful blows to the concept of the perfectibility of society; but having recorded that trauma the writers turned creatively in new directions.

These factors—the national sense of security and the still vibrant belief in the power of moral example as well as a heightened sense of social awarness brought on by the economic problems of the depression—are reflected in the two major war novels about the thirties, Hemingway's *For Whom the Bell Tolls* (1940) and James Jones's *From Here to Eternity* (1951). *For Whom the Bell Tolls* represents a way of dealing with war that emphasizes the importance of personal involvement rather than the larger futility of a particular operation. As Robert Jordan lies wounded waiting for the enemy to appear, he thinks, " 'I have fought for what I believe in for a year now. If we win here we will win everywhere. The world is a fine place and worth the fighting for and I hate very much to leave it. . . . I wish there was some way to pass on what I have learned though.' "[7] In this case the gesture Jordan makes is associated with a social cause which came to absorb the interests of writers in the thirties.

The problem of social justice, which Steinbeck considers on the national level in *The Grapes of Wrath,* is dealt with on the international scale in Hemingway's work. Where Frederick Henry's concept of war had been limited to the possibility of a solution imposed by military force, Robert Jordan's is ultimately pacifist. Henry accepts the idea that wars must be fought and the enemy must be defeated, that the doctrine of force is a continuing factor in human affairs. The mood of *For Whom the Bell Tolls* is that the war is accepted as an immediate necessity but one which may possibly be avoided in the future, not by imposing the will of the victor upon the vanquished but by appealing to the humanity of both parties. As one of Hemingway's wise peasants says to another, " 'We must teach them. We must take away their planes, their automatic weapons, their artillery and teach them dignity.' "[8]

The Spanish Civil War was the mirror image of the sort of war in which the United States usually became involved in the twentieth century: individuals volunteered to serve while the nation remained officially neutral. Since 1917 the tendency has been for the nation to get involved while individuals try to opt out. Allen Guttman has suggested that although the Spanish Civil War disturbed the part of the American public that was politically alert as no other event except the Great Depression itself, it also had a curiously satisfying quality. It was a war in which the natural man in the tradition of Thoreau and Whitman clearly opposed the forces of a mechanized society.[9] El Sordo defending his hill-top against the aircraft and Jordan blowing up the bridge to stop the tanks represent, in a way, the desires of a society anxious about the increasing regimentation of their own lives.

The differences between the themes of *From Here to Eternity* and *For Whom the Bell Tolls* illustrate the divergence in American attitudes toward warfare and the military establishment in the thirties. Hemingway's work deals with political and social issues on the international scale; the protagonist is a civilian and a liberal fighting essentially for social justice and a new order of arbitration in international affairs. Jones's hero Prewitt is a poor boy from Kentucky who enlists in the army strictly for personal reasons and serves efficiently without ever entertaining any larger social or political concepts. Stanley Cooperman has commented:

Part of this country's historic schizophrenia toward war and armies . . . was the conviction, often justified, that "joining up" was prima facie evidence of failure in responsible citizenship. Before World War I a man became a "regular" soldier—especially an infantry soldier—because there was nothing else he could do, or because he had been involved in legal, economic or social difficulties.[10]

In Prewitt's case the economic difficulties that force him into the army are not of his own making; as for so many other youths in the depression nothing else is available. The loss of freedom involved in enlisting, however, is not a source of unhappiness to Prewitt; the army offers him a mode of life perfectly suited to his personality. In telling Prewitt's story, Jones points up once again the essential difference between the military establishment as an institution and the fact of modern warfare. The despair of the

World War I novelists derived from their recognition of the absurd and uncontrollable nature of industrialized warfare. *From Here to Eternity* presents the other face of the coin. Here all is neat, comprehensible, orderly. It is a closed system far more perfect than the unpredictable peacetime civilian life—a social order based on the tidy categories of section, platoon, company, and regiment and guided by army regulations and daily orders. Even Prewitt's tragic fate is worked out with a classic neatness and economy like that of Billy Budd. Had he been in action, he might have been destroyed in any of the ghastly and useless ways experienced by the soldiers of World War I; in the controlled environment of the peacetime army his destiny evolves with perfect logic from the time he quits the Bugle Corps to the moment the MP's bullets stitch in echelon across his chest.

What Jones is celebrating in *From Here to Eternity* is the idea of the peacetime army, the joy of soldiering experienced by every man who has known peacetime service in a good unit. Prewitt's destruction is important and well handled, the love affairs are unlikely, the portraits of the officers are typically uncertain and exaggerated; but all these points fade into insignificance beside the evocation of life in the regiment. With a sureness of touch born of personal experience, Jones evokes the satisfactions of peacetime service: the pride in the traditions of the regiment, the sense of physical well-being deriving from a healthy life, the satisfaction of seeing the unit function with well-oiled proficiency, the joy of knowing that responsibility for one's actions has clearly defined limitations. It is this element that makes *From Here to Eternity* unique among American war novels. The other novelists speculate on war in abstract terms or struggle to render comprehensible the experience of modern war or turn away in ultimate rejection. Jones, and to some extent John Marquand in *Melville Goodwin*, are the only ones to deal with the ethos of the army as an enduring institution with a life and tradition of its own.

But the army Jones celebrates in *From Here to Eternity* exists in a state that is sociologically and militarily unreal. By a curious irony, Kipling's verse, which Jones chose as the epigraph to the novel, suggests perfectly the strength and weakness of prewar army life:

> I have eaten your bread and salt.
> I have drunk your water and wine.
> The deaths ye died I have watched beside,
> And the lives ye led were mine.

Kipling, once the voice of empire, is dominated by his own jingoism; in the light of modern circumstances his work verges on high camp. Yet both these elements—a patriotic jingoism and an atmosphere of camp—were fundamental to the attitudes of the old army. In these circumstances it is not surprising that, to the vast majority of the American people, the peacetime army simply did not exist; they were either unaware of its existence or indifferent to it. Commenting on the German submarine attack on the U.S.S. *Kearney* in which eleven crew members were killed on 17 October 1941, Robert E. Sherwood said,

This incident was taken pretty much as a matter of course by the American people who always have considered the men in their regular armed forces—Navy, Army, and, most of all, Marine Corps—as rugged mercenaries who signed up voluntarily, as do policemen and firemen, for hazardous service; it was, of course, tough luck when any of them were killed in the line of duty. . . . There was little or no self-identification of the normal American civilian with the professional American soldier or sailor.[11]

On the other hand, the regular army could not exist under conditions of modern war; the abrupt expansion of the forces in wartime dispersed the peacetime units and diluted their traditions and motivations out of existence. Thus, in *From Here to Eternity*, the joyous battle staged on the roofs of Schofield Barracks as the Japanese attack Pearl Harbor marks the end of an era in which the army could exist within the structure of society but separate from it. The army Jones glorifies never really reappeared in America; after World War II the permanent integration of the United States into world affairs and the events of the cold war brought about changes in the nature of the military establishment that were to remove permanently the distinctions on which the isolation and security of regimental life had been based.

PART TWO: 1939-1952

6. INTRODUCTION

When the American youth thought about the military establishment at all in the interwar period, the financial hardships he was experiencing could only have served to strengthen what Samuel P. Huntington has described as the traditional American view—derived from the Protestant ethic and the writings of Spencer, Fiske, and Sumner—that the armed forces were parasitical and wasteful.[1] Incidents such as the time in 1932 when an army detachment evicted the unemployed "bonus marchers" from Washington occasionally transformed contempt and indifference into rage. Tradition and the economic hardships of the depression caused military spending to be restricted during the interwar years and American military thinking to be focused on domestic rather than strategic matters. President Hoover reflected the national mood in a message to the Senate on 7 July 1930 on the subject of the London Naval Treaty when he expressed satisfaction over the limitations imposed on the building of warships; he was convinced that the money saved thereby would be of much more use in meeting domestic requirements, especially social welfare.[2] And the Social Service Research Council records that the primary peacetime concern of the armed forces was "to protect the lives and property of American nationals rather than to provide for national defense."[3] As a result of these attitudes, the strengths of the various services had deteriorated by 1940 to approximately the same point from which they had started in 1914.[4]

The sense of disgruntlement experienced by many Americans at the outcome of World War I found expression as early as 1920 in a series of articles by Sidney B. Fay in which he examined what he considered to be the real causes of America's entry into the war. The evidence provided by these articles and his later *The Origins of the World War* (1928) gave rise to the idea that the United

States had been duped into intervening in the European conflict. This argument also underlies many other works written in the decade of the twenties, including Harry Elmer Barnes's *The Genesis of the World War* (1926) and C. Hartley Grattan's *Why We Fought* (1929).[5] Samuel E. Morison says that the American people felt World War I had been caused by a competitive armaments policy, by fear of the unknown enemy, by profiteering on the part of bankers and munitions manufacturers, and by the United States' insistence on neutral rights.[6]

The widespread belief in the concept of the "merchants of death" coupled with the general feeling of hostility toward big business which resulted from the crash of 1929 help to explain the popular acclaim that greeted the formation of a committee headed by Senator Gerald P. Nye of North Dakota to investigate the armaments industry in 1935. There was nothing objective about Nye's approach; he had been attacking big business for years and had assumed from the outset of his investigation that "armaments races, international friction, and wars themselves were encouraged by munitions manufacturers and financiers in their quest for profits."[7] By the time his inquiry had ended in 1936 he was forced to abandon his belief that the munitions manufacturers were promoting international conflict; instead he came to realize that the federal government was at fault for actively promoting the munitions industry.[8] Despite this, the popular image of Nye as the man who exposed the merchants of death persists to this day, undoubtedly because it was established at a time when the public wanted a group on which it could fix the blame for a very disappointing war.

The reaction of the American public to the Spanish Civil War must also be assessed with caution, mainly because an exceptionally vociferous group of men actually participated in the war. Allen Guttman's contention that the war disturbed the American public as no other event of the thirties except the Great Depression itself[9] becomes less dramatic in the light of some statistics. The men who went to Spain tended to be drawn from a highly articulate group: writers, the politically aware, and adventurers. Although many of these men (like Hemingway) served actively for extended periods of time, others remained in Spain for only a few days or weeks. In subsequent reminiscences a very small experience of the war went a long way. The number of Americans who actually fought in the International Brigade was about 2,800;[10] although they are credited with fighting bravely and suffered appalling casualties,[11] their efforts were restricted almost entirely to a ten-month period in 1937. After the first spate of volunteers there were few replacements. The implication is that the war was vitally important to a tiny fraction of the population. Many others were disturbed by it but were far more anxious about problems at home. On the basis of the public opinion polls taken between 1936 and 1939 it has been observed: "Not until May, 1939, was the problem of keeping out of war, let alone any other issue involving foreign policy, listed as the most serious American problem."[12]

Not only were the American people indifferent to world strategy and preoccupied with domestic affairs, they became actively opposed to the prospect of involvement in another war as the decade of the thirties advanced. The news of the rise of German totalitarianism in Europe and the spread of Japanese imperialism in the Far East impinged with increasing force on the national consciousness, carrying with it the almost inevitable promise of war. To this uncomfortable threat the American people reacted by trying to legislate their way out of future military entanglements. The neutrality acts passed between 1934 and 1937 sought to plug the various gaps in United States foreign policy by which the country had drifted into the First World War. The 1934 act cut off credits to countries in default to the United States, thereby eliminating financial interest as a reason for involvement in a foreign war. The 1935 act authorized the President to prohibit all arms shipments to belligerents and to forbid American citizens to travel on belligerent vessels except at their own risk. The 1936 act forbade loans or credits to belligerents, and that of 1937 authorized the embargo of arms shipments and financial aid to participants in a civil war.[13] At home military appropriations were carefully labeled to avoid any misconceptions regarding the government's aggressive intentions; e.g., "evidence of the Roosevelt administration's policy was its rejection of a request for long-range bombers by the Army Air Force in 1938 on the ground that 'our national policy contemplates preparation for defense, not aggression.' "[14]

Despite the softness with which he had to tread in order to avoid arousing the suspicions of the anti-interventionists, President Roosevelt seems always to have thought of the United States in strategic terms. He was unhappy with the neutrality acts in 1937 because they placed the Spanish Republicans at a severe disadvantage, and later he refused to invoke them during the Chinese-Japanese conflict because they would have weighed unfairly against the Chinese. His approach to foreign policy was outlined in his "Quarantine" speech in Chicago on 5 October 1937: "There is a solidarity and interdependence about the modern world, both technically and morally, which makes it impossible for any nation completely to isolate itself from economic and political upheavals in the rest of the world";[15] he also urged a strict boycott against the trade of aggressor nations.

If Roosevelt had no illusions about the permanent involvement of the United States in world affairs, the attitudes of other Americans covered practically the whole spectrum of opinion. A random selection of the speeches made in 1940 and 1941 by leading figures reveals that many intellectuals and politicians recognized that the United States was committed to the Allied cause even well before Pearl Harbor.[16] Many of the younger intellectuals like Stephen Vincent Benét, Archibald MacLeish, McGeorge Bundy, and Walter Millis accepted and supported America's participation in the war,[17] in contrast to the attitude of the younger generation of 1917. Finally there were people like Henry L. Stimson, who still relied hopefully on geographic isolation as the basis for a policy of neutrality, and the America First Committee, in which men like Colonel Lindbergh felt that conflict with Germany would be both contrary to the United States' own best interests and a gratuitous interference in the affairs of a well-organized nation. Dorothy B. Goebel claims that the "majority of Americans supported 'aid short of war' as the best defense of America's interests and peace."[18] It is worth noting that the first wartime Roper poll taken in September 1939 revealed that 29.9 percent of the population desired strict neutrality including denial of assistance to the Allies—a figure too large to represent only America Firsters, communists, and fascist sympathizers. This hard core of strict isolationists remained intact throughout the war.[19]

Consequently, it is not surprising that the American people engaged in World War II in a spirit of glum resignation; for the most part, they saw it as a task that had to be accomplished in order that they might return to their civilian lives as quickly as possible. If the attitude of the American soldier in World War I was informed with the classic American attribute of idealism, that of the World War II soldier was marked chiefly by the other familiar American characteristics of pragmatism and realism. Yet the relative equanimity with which the American citizen faced the prospect of combat in 1941 and the almost total absence of emotional trauma in fiction about the war do not seem to have derived to any great extent from the experience of World War I. Most of the generation that provided the soldiers for World War II had been born after 1918; although they had perhaps read the works of Hemingway, Cummings, and Dos Passos, the first war was for them a vicarious experience. Malcolm Cowley has observed that the "Americans in World War II were tougher and more sophisticated than their fathers in 1918,"[20] but the emotional toughness with which they were endowed seems to have been a product of the social and economic difficulties experienced by the nation as a whole in the thirties:

[There was] a basic difference of attitude and response. . . . [This generation] had no need for glorious adventure nor relief from boredom. Their lives . . . had been spent in a world continually at war with itself. . . . They could remember nothing but domestic unrest, fumblings at peace conferences, Asiatic invasions, and South American revolutions. . . . They came to consciousness in the midst of breadlines, strikes, and milk riots.[21]

In the works of Mailer, Jones, Shaw, and many other novelists of the Second World War one sees the recurrent image of the young man who graduated from high school or college and, finding no opportunity for a career, drifted from one casual job to another as the years went by. To this generation the harsh experience of the depression seems to have permanently blunted the traditional American sense of idealism. Speaking of the riots that occurred wherever American troops were stationed in 1946, one sociologist observed: "The behavior of the men was . . . not only a repudiation of Army authority and military discipline but ultimately of the whole purpose of the war they fought to win."[22] As far as they were concerned, if the nation was in an economic cul-de-sac, then it was necessary to pass out through the bottleneck—even if it meant military service—in order to regain personal economic freedom and the opportunity to live a normal life. This assessment of the situation was reflected in the less emotional response to the war by the population as a whole. "The satisfaction that the United States took in the triumph of its arms between 1941 and 1945 was profound but, to one who can remember the delirium of 1918, remarkably sober."[23]

For the literature of the war the principal effects derived from the fact that the United States participated much more fully in World War II than it had in World War I. The war, especially in the Pacific, brought home to the American people a unique experience as a great power whose attitudes were influenced very little by those of the Allied countries. "The Pacific campaign changed all that for American novelists. This war was really theirs. . . . Looking back on the Pacific the Americans . . . built up a thorough and realistic war literature from the foundations, to make the genre their own, as if it had never existed before."[24]

One sees this new aspect of the American outlook reflected in the soldiers' attitudes toward friend and foe: where Cummings had admired "les poilus divins," Malcolm Cowley now observed that in World War II "the soldiers made little distinction among the occupied, the liberated, and the Allied countries, since the people in all of them were foreigners—that is, frogs, limeys, heinies, ginsoes, yellow bastards, wogs, flips or gooks."[25] The responsibility for carrying the burden of the war turned the American point of view inward; the more realistic concept of warfare with which the nation entered the conflict and the longer exposure to combat provided the opportunity for a set of fully developed attitudes to ripen and be recorded. These attitudes remain fairly consistent in many of the novels written from 1945 to 1956. Thus, although in the novels of World War II there is no chronological movement from idealism to despair as there had been in the literature of World War I, there does emerge a series of portraits—of the civilian soldier, the professional officer, the Jew—reflecting typically American responses to warfare and the military establishment.

7. THE CIVILIAN SOLDIER

American war novelists in general tend to be the bards of the enlisted man, sensitive to his woes and glories. This point is especially true if one accepts the premise that the reserve officer, in rejecting or ignoring the function of command, also falls into a category not much different from that of the private soldier; he draws a higher salary and wears a different insignia, but his outlook on the war and the regular military establishment approximates that of the enlisted man. Therefore, although the American novelist treats of both officers and men, the viewpoint of both groups is largely identical and varies only when the writer deals with either academy graduates or regular noncommissioned officers.

The characteristics shared by the protagonists of the World War II novels is a total lack of the crusading spirit. Where their World War I counterparts joined up to fight the Hun or to engage in an exciting adventure, they joined for purely practical or selfish reasons. In most cases they knew that the draft was hanging over them in any event and that by volunteering they could either alleviate the tension of waiting or seek some special status denied to draftees. In some cases, like that of Red Valsen in *The Naked and the Dead* (1948), the individual joined up because the army offered him employment after years of drifting. In others, like that of Willie Keith in *The Caine Mutiny* (1951), volunteering was a means of obtaining a commission in the navy instead of being sent to the infantry.

Only very rarely does one find a volunteer like Noah Ackerman in *The Young Lions* (1948) who actually is moved by a desire to fight against the Nazi regime. Occasionally a character like Jim Wilson in *So Little Time* (1943) or Danny Forrester in *Battle Cry* (1953) joins for patriotic reasons; but in contrast to the volunteers of World War I who saw "right and wrong, honor and dishonor, humanity and savagery facing each other . . . squarely across the trenches,"[1] it is considered bad form to parade one's reasons for joining. The business of enlisting is usually treated soberly and with a minimum of flag-waving. To the majority of the characters, however, the war has come as an onerous obligation enforced by the threat of the draft. For most of these men, wartime service was only another bump on the long road of misfortune their generation had already traveled; as William Bradford Huie observed, this very matter-of-factness deprived the soldier of a traditional source of morale: "This war . . . was never presented as a crusade—no music, no poems, no flags—and it's cruel to ask a man to risk his life in any war which isn't fought for the highest purpose."[2]

If the fictional World War II hero enlisted as a matter of necessity rather than for humanitarian or patriotic reasons, his objectives in the war were equally practical. During a conference with the Soviet Foreign Minister in the White House in 1942, President Roosevelt said that as a result of this war "he believed that a peace could be established and guaranteed for at least twenty-five years, or as long as any of his and Stalin's and Churchill's generation could expect to live."[3] In other words, this was not a war to end war or to introduce the millenium but to achieve the fairly realistic goal of immediate peace. This objective, or variations of it, is what the novelists suggest that the typical American pursued in World War II; the peace they sought was a peace in which they would have the opportunity for personal economic development rather than the culmination of a victorious crusade. In *The Naked and the Dead* Gallagher wants to get back to his career as a small-time politician, and Goldstein dreams of setting himself up in a welding shop in the Bronx. Eddie Slovik's letters to his wife are full of despair at the disruption of his domestic happiness and full of the agonized hope that he will survive to return to his wife and his job in a plumbing shop. Even the intellectuals like Keefer in *The Caine Mutiny* and Andrews in *Guard of Honor* (1948) pay practically no attention to the ideology of the war. Keefer wants to be the first to rush into print with his wartime experiences; Andrews, while serving loyally enough in a research squadron in Florida, cannot help feeling that his talents are being wasted and that time is passing him by.

If, in joining the armed forces, many characters are shown as following a path they hope will eventually bring them the opportunity for economic advancement in civilian life, others seek the same objective in a military career. Steve Maryk in *The Caine Mutiny* has been a fisherman all his life. To him the prospect of advancement as a career officer is primarily a matter of exchanging a hard and unrewarding life for one that offers security and social status. Similarly Major Dalleson, General Cummings's operations officer in *The Naked and the Dead,* is forced by his dream of a captaincy in the peacetime army to reluctantly take the initiative when he finds himself in the uncomfortable position of directing a battle during the general's absence. Neither Maryk nor Dalleson is a professional soldier in the sense that he has chosen a career in the armed forces for the sake of the military life itself. Those qualities that John Marquand attributes to Major General Melville Goodwin—i.e., acceptance of a long and stringent formative period, desire for command of troops in action, the willing exchange of financial welfare for the privileges of rank, living by a stern code of duty—do not form part of their makeup. They are professional soldiers only in the sense that they intend to spend their lives in the service.

In addition to the search for economic welfare, either in the armed forces or as a result of the advent of peace, an author occasionally suggests that one of his characters has joined up as a gesture in his search for social equality. In Merle Miller's *That Winter* (1948) Ted Hamilton, the fabulously rich misfit, finds a certain degree of acceptance in the army—both by his largesse and his personal courage—which he was never able to achieve either as a student before the war or as a businessman in the postwar period. In a sense Willie Keith hopes to achieve something similar in his wartime service. To Sergeant Julio Martinez in *The Naked and the Dead* the army represents a way to escape the stigma of his Mexican origin. After a youth filled with humiliation as a counter boy and farmhand, a sergeantcy in the United States Army offers a social status he could never attain by any other means. To relinquish it by leaving the army or being broken would mean returning to the status of a servant or wetback laborer. "Little Mexican boys also breathe the American fables. If they cannot be aviators or financiers or officers they can still be heroes."[4] This thought drives him forward even when he is in the grip of convulsive fear.

Finally the World War II novelists depict the individual who goes to war in search of experience. This sense of adventure was a common characteristic among the fictional heroes of World War I, but in the novels of the Second World War those characters who are seeking experience tend to be a good deal more sophisticated than their earlier counterparts. In 1917 the American youth was avid for adventure and for relief from the monotony of life at home. Europe, especially France, was the unknown country offering strange and sometimes illicit delights. Cummings, Lieutenant Henry, and John Andrews found a stimulation in Europe not greatly different in quality from that experienced by the average tourist. Mailer's Lieutenant Hearn, on the other hand, joins the army in search of data that will confirm his rather dismal view of human nature: "The only thing that interested him vitally was to uncover the least concealed quirks of any man or woman who diverted him. 'When I find the shoddy motive in them I'm bored.' "[5]

He has already been abroad; the simple excitements of foreign travel have no special attraction for him. Like most of the intellectuals in World War II fiction he seeks experience in the military service on a philosophical plane; the army brings together under unusual circumstances personalities that would not normally associate with one another and forces them to react with each other under stress. It is this bringing together and the subsequent reaction that Hearn wishes to observe. On a less disinterested level Thomas Keefer in *The Caine Mutiny* does exactly the same thing. His interest is primarily commercial, in that his service experience is rapidly transcribed into a novel which he rushes off to sell in New York as soon as the ship lands.

Saul Bellow in *Dangling Man* (1944) presents an even more subtle approach to the search for experience than that of Hearn or Keefer. Bellow's hero is the antithesis of military activists like Melville Goodwin in that he is given to an examination of every motive before he acts. He feels it is necessary for him to enlist because the burden of living without any form of regimentation (he has quit his job and has no other responsibilities) is driving him mad. Curiously for a writer whose tone is invariably that of the blundering but untouchable individualist, Bellow makes Joseph say that human beings always seek "the leash." "We are afraid to govern ourselves. . . . We soon want to give up our freedom. It is not even real freedom, because it is not accompanied by comprehension. . . . But we hate it."[6] In this context he is saying that the only type of experience the individual can stand is collective, externally directed effort, but he goes beyond this to offer what may be a subtle explanation of the motives of many Americans in joining up. Joseph says that he wishes to regard the war as an incident, an incident capable of killing him as a bacteria could kill him, but he also wants to be involved in it because it is a part of the common experience of his generation.[7]

A quite similar sentiment is expressed in Robert Lowry's *Casualty* (1946), an otherwise insignificant novel about a private in a photoreconnaissance unit in Italy. Private Hammond detests the army and the war but admits to himself that he did not seek to avoid military service as a conscientious objector because "he had wanted the experience if the rest of the world was to have it."[8] This desire for an introverted and almost tribal quality of experience is far removed from the purposes attributed to the American soldier in the fiction of World War I and is characteristic of a certain element in World War II fiction in that it hopes to find the significance of the war within the confines of American society, as it is represented in the armed forces, rather than in external contacts between Americans and foreigners. The soldiers in the works of Hemingway, Cummings, Dos Passos, and Cather see the war in terms of its impact on themselves as individuals and on Europe as a society; but in the novels of the Second World War the experience of war relates to American society as a group. It is rare that a novelist considers the effects of the war from the point of view of the English, the French, or the Italians. By the time World War II broke out, the American people, at least as they are portrayed in their literature, had overcome the Jamesian naiveté that led them to seek intellectual fulfillment in the Old World. By this time they are shown as being preoccupied with the problems of their own security and no longer overawed by the European presence.

What the American soldier hoped to achieve by military service must have been tempered by his first taste of training and combat. In varying degrees the novelists show the transformation of the individual from a resigned, if reluctant, draftee into a more or less aggressive combatant. For one thing the training process was less objectionable and far more realistic than it had been in World War I. The characters in the novels of Boyd, Stevens, and Dos Passos had recorded their disgust and disillusionment both with the treatment accorded them in the training camps and with the irrelevance of the material they were required to learn. Boredom and apathy are necessary concomitants of any enforced training program, especially when the audience is intelligent, moderately well informed, and accustomed to an easier mode of life; but the outlook of the trainee in the works of Wouk, Huie, Shaw, and Uris, if still antagonistic toward military routine, is at least not outraged or disgusted. Among those who enlisted out of selfish motives, like Willie Keith in *The Caine Mutiny*, a process of self-identification with the unit tends to take place; even Eddie Slovik, the most reluctant of soldiers, found himself unwilling to let the side down.

The appeal to the team spirit is perhaps the only positive motivation mentioned in the novels of World War II. Recognizing the dangers of an overblown propaganda campaign, the new emotional toughness of the American soldier, and the greater availability of factual information, "the trend from 1941 to 1945 was toward an avoidance of any form of overt appeal to the emotions [of the draftee]."[9] The negative motivation that moved the American civilian to become proficient and to fight bravely was the realization that victory was the only way out of the army. In *Guard of Honor* James Gould Cozzens says of the American soldier, "Brought within fighting distance of the enemy, he saw well enough that until those people over there were all killed or frightened into quitting, he would never get home. Very few of them accepted the notion that they fought, an embattled band of brothers, for noble 'principles.' "[10] Yet the experience of combat itself unexpectedly served to transform the draftee into a better motivated and more competent soldier. Ernie Pyle, who landed with the troops in North Africa, emphasizes this psychological effect of the campaign. Practically until the moment of landing, the troops thought only of going home with a whole skin; after the first engagement they began to think in terms of the necessity for more combat, of finishing out the war by defeating the enemy on the battlefield.[11]

This process from resentment to involvement may have been motivated by an ultimately selfish pragmatism, but it resulted in what seems to have been a deeper comradeship and loyalty to the unit than that described in the novels of World War I. Mattock, Chrisman in *Three Soldiers,* and Hicks in *Through the Wheat,* who go overseas starry-eyed with dreams of saving civilization, become disillusioned and isolated both from society at large and from their fellow soldiers. On the other hand, the fictional American soldier of World War II is shown as being reluctant, emotionally uncommitted, and rather cynical when he is drafted but becoming welded into the team by the experience of war. Willie Keith and Ted Hamilton, the rich dilettantes of *The Caine Mutiny* and *That Winter,* turn into fairly proficient soldiers, identifying themselves unashamedly with their fellow combatants. One of the fine minor novels of the war, Harry Brown's *A Walk in the Sun* (1944), shows a group of draftees as having become a smooth-working team under the pressures of war. With the platoon officer and senior NCOs dead or wounded, the platoon still functions competently and responsibly under the direction of one of the corporals in going on to take its objective. More important, there is no suggestion of the pessimism and despair common to characters in the novels of World War I, even though the platoon mission is extremely dangerous. Instead there is a sense of solidity, mutual confidence, and even affection deriving from the reliance of the members of the team upon each other. This effect is generally true of the novels of World War II; the avoidance of emotional propaganda, the nature of the basic training program, and the effect of the soldier's first taste of combat are shown as having a positive effect on the attitude of the draftee toward the unit in which he served, even while his knowledge of war and his revulsion against it deepened.

Among the civilian soldiers who had to make the transition to service life were the reserve officers, and they are usually portrayed as interlopers in a strange and hostile environment. Coming from every conceivable background—student, journalist, teacher, used-car salesman, fisherman—the fictional reserve officers illustrate once again that the concept of command and the exercise of arbitrary authority are distasteful to the American mind. They tend to ignore or avoid, as far as it is possible to do so, those functions that set the regular officer outside the accepted pattern of American mores and usually try to conduct themselves in accordance with the framework of civilian life. Where possible they assiduously cultivate the illusion that they hold no authority whatever, since they know that the exercise of authority will earn them the hatred of the troops. This situation was later parodied in Joseph Heller's *Catch-22* (1961) in the episode where Colonel Cathcart capriciously hands the task of squadron commander to Major Major Major: " 'You're the new squadron commander,' Colonel Cathcart had shouted rudely across the railroad ditch to him. 'But don't think it means anything, because it doesn't.' "[12] The promotion means nothing in terms of prestige, but it means everything in terms of human relations. Major Major Major is simultaneously burdened with the task of squadron administration and finds himself sent to Coventry because he has assumed a status that is distasteful to his compatriots: "Almost on cue, everyone in the squadron stopped talking to him and started staring at him. He walked through life self-consciously with downcast eyes and burning cheeks, the object of contempt, envy, suspicion, resentment and malicious innuendo everywhere he went."[13] His dilemma culminates in the mob scene that occurs when he tries to seek companionship on the basketball court. He allows himself to be beaten up rather than commit the ultimate faux pas of exercising arbitrary authority.

Because of the tendency of the reserve officer to equate command with fascism, Willie Keith misjudges the personalities of both De Vriess and Queeg, just as John Hersey in *A Bell for Adano* (1944) contrasts Major Joppolo's conduct with that of the regular army officers. Joppolo is very much the civilian in uniform—humanitarian, just, generous, democratic. He does not understand the complicated hocus-pocus of army routine, and his personality clashes with those of the combat officers General Marvin and Colonel Middleton, who are depicted as brutal, impatient vandals—not much better than the Germans. Joppolo is the typical reserve officer in that he is happiest when he can act as a more highly paid technician or manager and thereby avoid the responsibilities of command. Similarly Benny Carricker in *Guard of Honor* holds his commission by virtue of his technical competence as a flier, and Thomas Keefer in *The Caine Mutiny* thinks that his intellect entitles him to be an officer without being part of the hierarchy.

Very rarely do the substitutes adopt the outlook of the regular members of the team. In *Mister Roberts* (1946), Roberts is practically unique in American war literature in that "he wants to be in the war; he is powerfully drawn to the war and to the general desolation of the time."[14] It has already been noted that the desire to participate in the war as a national experience is one of the underlying motives attributed to the Americans who enlisted in World War II, but Roberts's attitude goes beyond this; he is unusual in that he actually wants to exercise command. The usual attitude of the reserve officer is that of Roberts's colleagues who, feeling ridiculous in the trappings of command, "renounced the role altogether." Their opinion of the service is summed up by Lieutenant Keefer, who describes the armed forces as a master plan designed by geniuses for execution by idiots, and by Al Mannix in *The Long March* (1953), who thinks of the radio code language as "gibberish, the boy-scout password which replaced ordinary conversation in the military world. To Mannix they were all part of the secret language of a group of morons, morons who had been made irresponsibly and dangerously clever."[15]

Perhaps the special place of the noncommissioned officer in American war literature also derives in part from the distinction between leadership and command. The professional officer makes himself repugnant by exercising the function of command; the reserve officer tends to be a more highly paid technician without the élan that could help make him a dynamic leader. The NCO, therefore, is usually depicted as fulfilling the function of a team captain. In the American sporting tradition the team captain may lead but must not command, and he usually leads by a display of virtuosity. In many cases the NCO is an awesome figure capable of making or breaking the enlisted man without the knowledge of the unit's officers; as long as his professional competence is readily evident to the troops, he holds them in his thrall. He is in the fortunate position of stimulating the American respect for knowhow without having any of the distasteful militaristic or social distinctions of the West Point officer. James Jones's First Sergeant Warden is the archetype of the NCO in American fiction—omniscient, pragmatic, murderous; he shares these qualities with Mailer's Sergeant Croft, Shaw's Sergeant Rickett, and Harry Brown's Sergeant Halverson. To the troops these men are all clearly distinguished from the officers and yet isolated from the enlisted men by their single-minded devotion to the business of killing.

For the professional soldier like Melville Goodwin or Sergeant Croft the war is the culmination of his career, but for the great majority of characters in American fiction the war is seen in contrast to the individual's past life. The standard thematic device of the World War II novelist is to project the soldier's life against the backdrop of war. In the World War I novels the reader knows nothing about the background experiences of the characters. Only the sketchiest information is provided about where Henry, Andrews, Fuselli, Hicks, or Gilligan came from or what their previous experiences had been. They are treated not so much as individuals as composite expressions of the national will. Their stories begin from the time when they volunteer, in keeping usually with the overpowering American mood of idealism, and their reaction to the war is seen not so much as a product of their backgrounds as of the war itself. In the World War II novels, on the other hand, the war is a backdrop rather than a medium; it provides the screen on which are projected some further episodes in an already fairly complete history of the individual's life. In *The Naked and the Dead, A Bell for Adano, The Caine Mutiny, From Here to Eternity*, and *The Young Lions*, each author devotes a large part of the book to those events in the soldier's previous environment that influence his conduct in the armed forces.

Aside from establishing the fact that the enlisted man is essentially a civilian at heart whose prime desire is to get out of the army, this introduction of background material and shift in the relationship between the soldier and the battle is fundamental to the novelists' changing perception of the place of war in society. In the First World War, America's first real bloodletting against an external enemy, it was important and in fact sufficient to record the trauma of an idealistically motivated nation plunged into a mechanized slaughter. By developing the individual soldier's past life in detail and placing it in juxtaposition to the war, the authors of World War II novels provide the basis for an understanding of the point of view of the enlisted man as a person rather than as the symbol of a national outlook, which he tended to be in World War I fiction.

The revulsion at the endless slaughter expressed in the novels of World War I was in keeping with the sentiment of the whole western world; in the novels of the Second World War the element of disillusionment is less significant. The war presents different problems to different characters—problems which must be worked out in keeping with their special personalities. Thus, as in the title of Ned Calmer's book, the war is *The Strange Land*—a land with entirely new and different values and standards of conduct to which men react in various ways. Generally the atmosphere of war affects them like LSD or alcohol, heightening and emphasizing the characteristics the individual already possesses; the brave become braver, the cowardly more cowardly, the brutal more brutal.

Perhaps the prime question that was answered differently in the two wars was the question of the relationships existing between the individual, his own country, and the enemy. In the context of World War I, initially at least, the enemy was very clearly defined.

He was the Hun, and it could be taken for granted that any American youth regardless of his background would wish to fight against him. In the novels of the Second World War the enemy is rarely seen and only occasionally identified solely as the Germans or the Japanese. Instead the enlisted man more and more frequently expresses his resentment against "them"; it is implied that the "they" who are responsible for the war and for the enlisted man's misfortunes are governments in general and that one is not much better than another. Eddie Slovik's recurring cry in his letters to his wife is "Why did they have to do this to us?" When Al Mannix in *The Long March* sees a young Marine who has been killed in a training exercise, he murmurs weeping, " 'Won't they ever let us alone, the sons of bitches?' "[16] The barely articulated resentments of Valsen and Gallagher in *The Naked and the Dead* are directed not against the Japanese but against the "fugged up army." The defeat of Germany holds no promise of peace for the soldiers in *A Walk in the Sun*. Private Archimbeau wryly expects to be fighting the Battle of Tibet in 1958, having fought his way across Germany, the Balkans, the Middle East, and northern India by that time. All these characters reflect the increasing cynicism of the American citizen in regard to the purposes for which a war is fought, a process which culminates in Yossarian's decision that the war is a plot by both sides to murder him.

The fact that war itself, not any given nation, represents the real threat to human happiness was capable of special dramatization in those novels dealing with service in the Air Force. Some years later John Hersey was to take a line from a poem by William Butler Yeats as the motif for his novel about a bomber crew in England: "Those that I fight I do not hate."[17] For the fliers the differences between war and peace as modes of existence were more sharply apparent than ever before in history, because they alternated between both modes daily. For them there was no time to forget the blessings of peace or to become accustomed to war. Furthermore, the war as seen from the air assumed a personality of its own. An artillery observer in one novel muses, "Had he thought once that war had an issue? Anti-fascism perhaps? Under aerial observation, war shed issues. War was Fact, Thing-in-Itself, Existence sheer beyond argument; it spoke from the Rapido and beyond. 'I AM THAT I AM,' it declared. . . . 'I AM MY OWN JUSTIFICATION.' "[18] Under these circumstances it is easy to understand why, in a later novel of the absurd, Yossarian treats the institution of war as his prime enemy and the American officers of his own squadron as the representatives of that enemy.

If combat raised special problems for the civilian who suddenly found himself cast as a soldier, the occupation of conquered countries presented him with problems that were all the more acute because of the nature of the society from which he had come. The dilemma of the conqueror was essentially that the civilian-minded American, whose origins lay in a comparatively naive and simple society, was forced to deal with hardened veterans of military and political warfare whose origins lay in an old, complex society. The American was faced with the necessity of maintaining his perspective despite his own absolute power, his lack of experience, and the subtle blandishments of a people prepared to do anything in order to survive.

To Major Joppolo in *A Bell for Adano* the problem is relatively simple. Armed with his experience as a clerk in the New York City Hall and a touching faith in the power of American-style democracy to bring out the best in everyone, he sets about the task of bringing the town of Adano into the twentieth century. Joppolo's downfall is a result of the capriciousness of a regular army officer and his own democratic steadfastness, but in other American war novels the problems of the conqueror are treated more subtly. In David Davidson's *The Steeper Cliff* (1947), an American lieutenant is charged with the task of screening applicants for journalistic posts in the new German society. Lieutenant Cooper has to face the problem of judging men who may be his intellectual and moral superiors, a problem rendered more acute by his awareness of a degree of cowardice and blood-guilt in himself; his reaction to the situation is almost neurotic. Generally where the novelist deals with the American soldier facing the moral responsibilities of the occupation, the portrait is not a favorable one. Willa Cather was the first to perceive the unfortunate effect that removal of the usual moral restraints could have on the American; her theme is made more explicit in John Horne Burns's *The Gallery* (1947), which depicts the Americans as a barbarian horde invading and debauching a civilized country.

The same inverted Jamesianism is carried out in Alfred Hayes's *The Girl on the Via Flaminia* (1949): the American soldier, seeking a simple easy relationship with an Italian girl and not bothering to inform himself of the possible consequences, sets in motion a train of events that combine to destroy the girl. His problem is typically American in that he does not use force to gain his ends but makes the mistake of trying to reduce a human relationship to a simple bartering operation and being absolutely baffled by the complications that subsequently arise. He feels his situation to be absurd: on the one hand he has a premonition of his own inevitable destruction ("Hope and possibility and illusion had begun even then to vanish, and more and more he had let the idea of his own extinction become part of the way he lived."),[19] and on the other hand his status as conqueror prevents him from forming any meaningful relationship with the Italian people.

The American soldier is usually shown to be particularly unsuited, because of his democratic beliefs and rather simple outlook, to the task of ruling occupied countries; but the effects of combat itself were not always uniformly bad, as they had been in the novels of World War I. The tactics employed in the second war avoided the wholesale slaughter of the first and gave the draftee some opportunity to identify himself with an efficient team and to gain a sense of accomplishment as he carried out his duties. Willie Keith attains a degree of maturity from his service on the *Caine;* Michael Whitacre in *The Young Lions* sees courage and selflessness for the first time; John Hersey in *Into the Valley* (1943) recognizes the bravery and competence of the Marines on Guadalcanal. Occasionally, in a novel like Robert Bowen's *The Weight of the Cross* (1951) which deals with the experiences of an American sailor in a Japanese prison camp, the emphasis is on the fact that a man can survive under a ruthless system and thereby undergo a process of spiritual evolution. The despairing tone of *The Naked and the Dead* represents only one facet of the national reaction to war; in many other novels World War II provides a basis of experience from which the Americans could evolve their own attitude toward warfare as an institution.

8. THE PROFESSIONAL OFFICER

For all the vast numbers of officers produced by the American war effort, the nature of the officer and his function remained enigmas with which the American novelist struggled unsuccessfully. The glaring weaknesses of Norman Mailer's *The Naked and the Dead* (1948) derive largely from a very typical American inability to comprehend the character of the professional officer. It might even be fair to say that *The Naked and the Dead* is not a novel at all; it could be described as several brilliant short stories mired in a swamp of turgid ideological discourse. When Mailer deals with the enlisted man or describes scenes of combat (as in the assault crossing of the river by the Japanese or the heart-stopping terror of Sergeant Martinez's night patrol through the Japanese lines) he is unsurpassed; and he is masterful in his descriptions of the agony of weariness and discomfort experienced by the infantry soldier; but when he attempts to deal with the viewpoint and motivation of the officer, the narrative falters and his living characters become mouthpieces for a political dialogue. Mailer seems to be a novelist of action rather than motivation. The motivations he ascribes to his characters—Cummings for becoming a professional soldier, Croft for wanting to climb the mountain—seem to be contrived, but when he describes Cummings commanding the division or Croft leading the platoon his touch is sure.

Mailer is not alone among American novelists in this incapacity. The English war novel normally deals with the officer rather than the enlisted man, but the American war novel almost never takes this point of view. In England not only the World War I novelists like Graves, Ford, and Sassoon deal primarily with the officer, but many popular World War II novelists like Evelyn Waugh and Eric Williams do so as well. In the whole range of American war novels only one or two writers adopt the point of view of the professional officer and only a handful take the point of view of the reserve officer. This indicates a profound divergence between American and European attitudes toward the military establishment and seems to be worthy of examination in some detail.

When it does become necessary to describe the officer and his function, many American writers share C. Wright Mills's belief that since the military leaders have been traditionally drawn either from the financially or politically influential groups or from circles sympathetic to these groups and therefore conservative in outlook, they identify their interest with the maintenance of the status quo.[1] Such a creed is of course anathema to the traditions of American liberalism and helps explain the veiled hostility inherent in the fictional portait of the professional officer, but it is also important to keep in mind that America is one of the few western societies where the officer class has no place in the scheme of things. The European soldier responds instinctively to rank because it is part of his cultural heritage to do so; the American soldier sees the officer as someone no better than himself who has been arbitrarily invested with the authority to abuse his subordinates. Surprisingly, for all the criticism of Willa Cather's war scenes and characterization of the American soldier as a spirtual Boy Scout, she seems to have understood the function of the officer better than many of her male counterparts who had seen active service. Her description of Claude Wheeler's decisiveness and competence in the face of a German attack is much more the portrait of a good officer than is, for example, Lieutenant Henry's hysterical shooting down of the Italian sergeant who refused to help him with his ambulance.

The concept of command is so foreign to the American mind that Mailer's Lieutenant Hearn has to painfully work it out for himself as though it were an innovation. On the one hand he sees only the naked fascism of General Cummings or Sergeant Croft: "Croft had the wrong kind of command, a frightening command";[2] on the other hand he knows leadership only as the sort of crude, artificial bonhomie practiced by his father in his relationships with other businessmen. Hearn thinks that a humane and intelligent approach to the enlisted men "would end by confusing and annoying them. Croft they would obey, for Croft satisfied their desire for hatred, encouraged it, was superior to it, and in turn exacted obedience. The realization depressed him."[3]

At least one sociologist has made the distinction between two main categories of officers—the heroic leader and the military manager: "The military manager reflects the scientific and pragmatic dimensions of war-making; he is the professional with effective links to civilian society. The heroic leader is a perpetuation of the warrior type, the mounted officer who embodies the martial spirit and the theme of personal valor."[4] In the film version[5] of Pierre Boulle's *The Bridge on the River Kwai* (1954) both of these types of officer are depicted; in a sense the bridge is the medium by which a certain rapport is finally achieved between them. The British Colonel Nicholson is managerial-minded to the point of lunacy (e.g., he contends that the order to surrender at Singapore implied that he and his men were forbidden to escape); Colonel Saito represents the warrior mentality who characteristically urges the prisoners to "be happy in your work" rather than telling them to do it as a duty. His approach to a problem is emotional where Nicholson's is rational. The American Shears thinks they are both mad—not, like Clipton, because of a humanitarian bias but because to him Saito's warrior code is merely a form of fanaticism and Nicholson's superb bridge is so much wasted effort.

Each of these two outlooks is either foolish or impractical to the pragmatic American mind; certainly the warrior mentality is incomprehensible to Americans in general. The wildly eccentric officer, whose idiosyncracies give him a special appeal in the eyes of the troops and who appears fairly frequently in European war literature (for example, Nicholson in *The Bridge on the River Kwai* or Waugh's mad brigadier in *Officers and Gentlemen*), rarely appears in the pages of the American war novel. There madness is no laughing matter; it endangers the smooth functioning of the organization. The real-life General Patton—whose personality resembled that of other famous warriors like Skorzeny, Lovat, and Montgomery—was the source of considerable uneasiness to the military hierarchy. When mental aberration does appear in fictional officers like Queeg or Yossarian, it is presented as neurosis rather than *poiesis;* both the individual's fictional counterparts and the audience see him as a fit subject for psychoanalysis. Thus the reserve captain Al Mannix in William Styron's *The Long March* (1953) fails to be inspired by Colonel Templeton's gung-ho decision to march the battalion thirty-six miles back to camp after a week in the field, and the manifestation of the warrior spirit in even so admirable a character as Melville Goodwin is a source of some consternation to the civilians he meets.

Not only the personality of the warrior but the character and function of the professional soldier in general mystify the American mind. It has been remarked that the American war novelist takes the point of view of the professional officer only in extremely rare instances; perhaps one or two novels in the entire canon are seen directly through the eyes of an academy graduate. In every other case the author has felt it necessary to interpose an interpreter between the officer and the audience. The interpreter is frequently a writer, editor, or intellectual—someone who is trained to present unusual phenomena to the public and is capable of providing the necessary focus and point of view on military life. Thus Melville Goodwin is seen through the eyes of news commentator Sidney

Skelton; General Beal in *Guard of Honor* (1948) through the eyes
of either Nathaniel Hicks (an editor) or Judge Ross; Queeg through
the eyes of Willie Keith; General Cummings in *The Naked and
the Dead* from the point of view of Robert Hearn. The frequent
use of the civilian intellectual to provide focus in the war novel
suggests that the military hierarchy and mode of life are incomprehensible to the civilian mind unless they are recast in specifically
nonmilitary terms; the distinction between military and civilian
modes of life is too broad to be bridged even in wartime when
many civilians are involved.

The portrait of the professional officer, even modulated and
rendered comprehensible by the intellectual commentator, varies
considerably from one writer to another. Marquand and Cozzens
are definitely condescending. They see the officer as a brave and
competent craftsman, a man of action, but not very bright. Sidney
Skelton can say admiringly of Melville Goodwin, "There was a
metal in him that life had never tarnished, though it possessed a
confusing luster for people like Dottie Peale and me";[6] but he also
thinks that "you had to be caught young, or you had to be a boy
at heart, to acquire the military mind,"[7] and he spends most of
his time trying to keep General Goodwin from making a fool of
himself in his relations with the public. Similarly, in *Guard of
Honor* Cozzens gives an admiring analysis of the process by which
General Beal decided to save himself from the Japanese on Bataan
and of his skill and decisiveness as an officer, but he also portrays
the key members of Beal's staff as toiling to prevent the general's
capriciousness from bringing chaos on himself and his command.

Norman Mailer and James Michener see the professional officer
as an intelligent fascist who looks forward to a world dominated by
the puritanical virtues of the academy. In *Tales of the South
Pacific* (1947) Michener merely implies that there exists a dislike
and resentment of "certain supercilious traits . . . in Annapolis
graduates," but his Admiral Tarrant in *The Bridges at Toko-ri*
(1952) is a duplicate of Mailer's General Cummings—equally incredible and holding the same reactionary views about the decadence of civilian life. In the fictional portrait of the professional
officer it is the quality of ruthlessness which underlies the novelists'
distrust, especially since it is not the familiar ruthlessness of the
financially motivated businessman but rather that which springs
from a desire for power. The novelists are uneasy and suspicious
in the presence of a motivation that is basically unselfish, even if it
is inexorable, and they frequently portray the officer as willing to
sacrifice every other consideration for the smooth functioning of
the system. Like so many other aspects of his book, James Jones's
Colonel Tall in *The Thin Red Line* (1962) is a composite of the

attitudes of the novelists of World War II. Tall's ruthlessness has the same inscrutable quality as that of General Cummings in *The Naked and the Dead* or that of JoJo Nichols, the Chief of the Air Staff's personal hatchetman in *Guard of Honor*. In *The Execution of Private Slovik* (1954) William Bradford Huie says that Generals Eisenhower, Cota, and Rudder were "convinced of their soldiers' creed that *an able-bodied citizen who won't fight for his country doesn't deserve to live.*"[8] Of General Cota in particular Huie says, "He is everything that West Point strives to to create: a reliable instrument for the preservation of the United States . . . a man who can fashion and use reliable instruments for the large-scale slaughter of this nation's enemies . . . an individual whose vocabulary has one key word: DUTY."[9]

If many novelists tend to be uneasy in the presence of the professional officer's awesome capacity for ruthless action, they also reveal a typically American admiration for his professional competence as a "manager of violence," in Harold Lasswell's phrase. As Norman Podhoretz has accurately observed, Mailer is hard-pressed to keep General Cummings and Sergeant Croft from running away with *The Naked and the Dead* for the simple reason that their "strength, courage, drive and stamina" make them infinitely preferable, in the American mind, to the whining defeatism of the other characters in the novel.[10] In *The Caine Mutiny* (1951) Willie Keith is forced, for similar reasons, to modify his first contemptuous estimate of Captain de Vriess. After the arrival of a new officer to replace Maryk as captain of the *Caine,* "Willie's vision of the mutiny as a triumph of Reserve heroism over neurotic Academy stupidity languished; the Academy was back in charge, and master of the situation."[11] It is this willingness and ability to take charge that Sidney Skelton admires so much in Melville Goodwin, in that it contrasts so strongly with his own civilian tendency to drift with the tide of events and to compromise with life, just as Judge Ross is moved to admiration and respect by the depth of General Nichols's comprehension and his calm assurance. Even Ross is occasionally dismayed by the capriciousness of fate, but Nichols remains self-confident and unperturbed in the face of every mischance.

Occasionally a writer will express admiration for the physical courage of the academy officers, as Allen Matthews does in *Assault* (1947)—reportage of the first ten days of the Iwo Jima campaign; more characteristically the quality to which the American mind responds is the courage to take decisions rather than the courage required for physical combat. Thus in *Guard of Honor* General Nichols is treated admiringly even though he has never been in action, while the war hero Lieutenant Colonel Carricker is treated

as an oaf. William Haines's *Command Decision* (1947) is similarly a study of the courage of decision; in this case the central figure,
General Dennis, opts to send his bomb group against three different
heavily defended targets even though his action will probably draw
censure from Congress. In *The Young Lions* (1948) Irwin Shaw
concedes that generals must match their "moral strength and intellectual ingenuity with their colleagues and antagonists."[12] Shaw's
General Emerson shares the mystical quality of Mailer's General
Cummings, Cozzens's General Nichols, and Marquand's General
Grimshaw; he is described as "a General with a face full of tragedy
and authority, whom you could not refuse anything."[13] Here as
elsewhere the emphasis is on authority rather than physical courage, and it is a type of authority that derives in part from the aura
of mystery surrounding the professional officer; the retreat into the
monastery had paid dividends in a curious but important way.
The officers who appeared in the novels of World War I were usually reserves and usually below the rank of major; in the literature
of World War II the novelists grappled with the problem of the
general officer whose apparent fascism was disturbingly counterbalanced by those qualities of competence and aplomb that draw
an instinctive response from the American mind.

9. THE JEW IN THE AMERICAN WAR NOVEL

For Americans in general the experience of World War II was broader than that of World War I in that it touched every income level and every ethnic group, but it had a special significance for one segment of American society—the Jews. Alfred Kazin refers to 1945 as a "pivotal year" in the history of the Jewish writer in America: the year in which the Jew became able to form part of the "modern movement" by expressing his cultural heritage as part of the larger intellectual scene. At this point, as the war provided subject matter for writers like Wouk, Bellow, and Mailer, "The Jewish writer . . . had particular reason to feel that this most terrible of all events in Jewish history bound him more closely to every fundamental question of human nature in Europe's self-destruction";[1] i.e., in the same year that the Jewish writer emerged from the intellectual ghetto he was faced with questions that were not only national but international in scope.

Beginning with *From Here to Eternity* (1951) a high proportion of the war novels deal with the special problem of the Jew in the armed forces. James Jones examines the problem as it existed even before the outbreak of hostilities, but he does not acknowledge that a marked degree of anti-Semitism exists in the American armed forces. His point of view is that some Jews draw criticism and abuse by a certain self-pitying attitude. Certainly in *From Here to Eternity* there is no evidence of overt anti-Semitism; Corporal Bloom's problems arise from his almost paranoid belief that the world is set against him.

On the other hand, it seems fair to say that the armed forces presented a multifaceted problem to the American Jew. The characteristics normally attributed to the race in fiction (a desire to be liked, a powerful sense of tradition and community life, an awareness of the suffering of the race as a long-standing fact, and a sense of cultural superiority to the Gentiles) practically guaranteed that they would come into collision with the mode of life in the army. The impersonality of the army would make it difficult for them to feel that their efforts were appreciated; the dispersal of their numbers into the vastness of the armed forces would deprive them of a sense of kinship and mutual contact; the normal military harshness in dealing with recruits could easily be misinterpreted as anti-Semitism; and the necessity of taking orders from the average soldier would offend people even less sensitive than those who were aware of a cultural heritage reaching back for thousands of years.

In *Dangling Man* (1944) Saul Bellow describes his hero's brooding, inactive, introspective existence, which is diametrically opposed to the activism and optimism of, say, John Marquand's General Melville Goodwin and is the root of his uneasiness as he faces the nonintellectual army milieu. Furthermore, like Al Mannix in William Styron's *The Long March* (1951), Joseph equates the professional soldier with the opportunist: "Many men carry their ambitions over from civilian life and don't mind climbing upon the backs of the dead, so to speak. It's no disgrace to be a private, you know.' "[2] And he almost perversely refuses to recognize that the role of the officer is one of responsibility as well as privilege: "As I see it, the whole war's a misfortune. I don't want to raise myself through it.' "[3] For a writer whose work is normally balanced by a sardonic awareness that the physical world usually overwhelms the world of the intellect in any case, Bellow is curiously gloomy in dealing with the prospect of serving in the armed forces. His whole outlook is summed up in the moment when, listening to a record during the weeks prior to being called up, Joseph says, "Its sober opening notes, preliminaries to a thoughtful confession, showed me that I was still an apprentice in suffering and humiliation. I had not even begun. I had, furthermore, no right to expect to avoid them";[4] later he adds, "I would rather be a victim than a beneficiary."[5] In this attitude the fact of German or American anti-Semitism played no part, and yet it was an attitude which could never be made compatible with life in the army.

If the Jew had this inherent tendency to be at odds with military life, the situation was rendered vastly more complex both by the acknowledged anti-Semitism of many Americans and by the special horrors of the Nazi regime. The German atrocities against the Jews placed a special obligation on the American jew to fight against the Nazis, but once he had enlisted or been drafted he found himself in a context that was fundamentally inimical to his way of thinking. He also found himself forced into the ironic position of trying to fight against German anti-Semitism when the people with whom he served very frequently showed that they were anti-Semitic too. Robert Sherwood made this comment on the invidious position of the Jew in America at the outbreak of World War II:

In the more violent isolationist arguments was the ugly undercurrent of accusation that what the country faced was a Jewish plot to get us into war. Lindbergh eventually brought this out into the open with his statement that the only people who favored American intervention were the Roosevelt family, the British and the Jews. Obviously, the Jewish community had ample reason to be anti-Nazi, but it was by no means unanimous in opposition to isolationism. There were Jews, particularly on the upper economic levels, who supported the America First Committee because their fear of anti-Semitism in America far transcended their resentment of Nazi barbarism in Europe.[6]

The irony of this situation has been exploited in many of the novels of the Second World War, especially those of Wouk, Shaw, Mailer, Martha Gellhorn, and Merle Miller. In *The Naked and the Dead* (1948) Mailer's two Jewish soldiers function as small cogs in the large divisional machine which is under the control and direction of a man who is essentially a fascist. Their efforts to counteract the inherent prejudice of their fellow soldiers drives them to special efforts, all the more ironic for being futile. Goldstein makes a superhuman effort to carry Wilson—a Southern cracker—back to the beach after he is wounded, only to have Wilson die en route; Roth is stung into a last effort on the march by the epithet "you Jew bastard." Yet even as he forces himself to attempt the suicidal leap across a mountain chasm he realizes that his death will not influence the ingrained prejudice of men like Gallagher: "If he refused to jump, Croft would have to come back. The patrol would be over. . . . But the platoon wouldn't understand. They would jeer him, take relief from their own weakness in abusing him. His heart was filled with bitterness."[7]

Irwin Shaw, especially in *The Young Lions* (1948), has been much more obvious in handling this theme. The fanatic young German, arch-enemy of the Jews, is named Christian; the young Jewish-American soldier is named Noah ("the one who was saved"), even though ironically he is killed at the very end of the book. His avenger is called Michael (the avenging angel of the Old Testament), and the American officer who sternly prohibits acts of anti-Semitism among the newly liberated inmates of a German concentration camp is named Captain Green. In keeping with traditional Jewish pessimism there might be an additional irony in the fact that the Jewish soldier is destroyed while the hedonistic, dissolute Gentile survives; the implication is that although in this war Noah was killed by Christian, the events of the war served to open the eyes of men like Michael and to establish the authority of officers like Green. However, of Noah's aggressive defense of his rights, Kazin has observed, "The Jew as scapegoat and outsider is a perennial theme in our history; but the Jew as militant sacrifice, as the hero of death, impatient of complexity, is a new feature."[8] He adds that this is not a particularly satisfying response to the problem of the Jew vis-à-vis American anti-Semitism, mainly because it tends to oversimplify and evade the problem.

The idea that the armed forces may represent the best hope of the Jews is also fundamental to the much-discussed coda to *The Caine Mutiny* (1951). Herman Wouk initially shows Greenwald, the clever Jewish lawyer, as banking on the inherent anti-Semitism of the military establishment. When he discusses the court martial with Steve Maryk, he reckons his Jewishness to be an advantage in the defense because the court will tend to overcompensate in his favor in order to avoid any real or imagined charge of anti-Semitism. Thus in a sense the emotional connotations of the German atrocities help sink Commander Queeg. Yet in the party that takes place later to celebrate Maryk's acquittal, Greenwald reverses his stance and pays tribute to the regular armed forces for having saved America's Jews from the fate of the European community.

As in the case of *The Young Lions,* the fact that one of the protagonists is a Jew is central to Martha Gellhorn's *The Wine of Astonishment* (1948). In this case the character Jacob Levy is initially not influenced one way or another by the fact of his Jewishness. He thinks of himself only as an American private. The war takes on a special significance, however, when he visits Dachau after the German surrender and is so disturbed by what he sees there that he runs amok with a jeep and kills three German civilians. He is seriously injured in the accident himself; symbolically his great physical beauty is permanently marred. His action typifies the dilemma of the American Jew: he finds that the war which has ostensibly been won has not eradicated the special evil of anti-Semitism, and he finds it impossible to direct his rage against an enemy who he knows is guilty. The three Germans he killed may or may not have been enemies of his race. Like Roth in *The Naked and the Dead,* he senses the futility of his action even while he feels compelled to act.

This frustrating realization that the enemy is both omnipresent and invisible brings various reactions in the Jewish characters in the different war novels. Some, like Roth, make a despairing or violent gesture against the whole non-Jewish world. Others, like Lew Colinsky in Merle Miller's *That Winter* (1945), anglicize their names when they return from the war and try to withdraw at least momentarily from the struggle. Finally there are those like Captain Stein in James Jones's *The Thin Red Line* (1962) and Jacob Epp in Mark Harris's *Something about a Soldier* (1957) who form the spearhead of the antimilitarist tendency in the war novels of the absurd which began to appear in the late fifties. Jacob especially rejects service in the American armed forces for reasons that spring from his position as a Jew, and he draws the strength to endure his treatment in the stockade from the cultural heritage of his race, just as his particular humanism is colored by his Jewish background. The implication is that the moral strength required to stand against the accepted code of conduct of western society—a code which seems compulsively directed toward self-destruction—springs from the heritage of an older and much-abused society. It is worth noting that, along with Jacob and Captain Stein, Joseph Heller's Yossarian the Assyrian is a Semite. Just as Faulkner in his treatment of southern society looks to the Negro's enduring qualities of patience, humor, and compassion—forged through a long history of adversity—to eventually supersede the sterility and selfishness of the Anglo-Saxon ruling class, so the war novelists ultimately turn to another maligned expatriate group for those qualities that seem to offer an adequate response to the prospect of universal destruction.

10. ASSESSMENT

In summary it could be said that the American novelists of World War II attributed a pragmatic and realistic outlook to the fictional soldier. Most of the writers based their novels on the active service they had seen during the war and were qualified by their experiences to treat a broader spectrum of military life than were the earlier group of novelists; but if they did treat such widely diversified aspects as the political and ethnic facets of the war and saw the soldier both as combatant and conqueror, the individual author tended to have a narrower outlook than his World War I counterpart. There is some bias toward a "platoon cosmology" with a few principal characters and a couple of dozen caricatures,[1] especially among those novelists who felt unable to handle the whole scope of the war and yet considered that the actions of a single individual would be insignificant. In other words, these authors sought to recreate the melting-pot atmosphere and to express a multiplicity of viewpoints without going beyond the manageable bounds of a section or a platoon.

Where the drama of the World War I novel derived from the element of shock arising out of the new and horrifying experience of war, the World War II novelists "lack such a point of view, for they have not found in war sufficient contrast with the culture in which they grew up."[2] Paradoxically, one result of this situation is that "this generation of writers escapes in most instances from the 'lost generation' idea, despite a lack of feeling that we have seen the end of war."[3] Their style, like Harry Brown's in *A Walk in the Sun* (1944), tends to be firm, unemotional, and realistic. In this it differs from the hyterical tone and the mockery of the absurdity of war characteristic of much World War I writing. The tone of the World War II novelists becomes cynical over the materialistic interpretations of the origins of the war rather than over the emotional shock of misplaced idealism or the horror of mechanized slaughter. A character in *The Gallery* (1964) says, "And what was this war really about? I decided that it was because most of the people of the world didn't have the cigarettes, the gasoline, and the food that we Americans had."[4]

In at least one sense the question of the place of war in human affairs supplies a standard by which the novels of World War II can be divided into two categories. In one category are the works of those novelists—Mailer, Brown, and Jones—who see the brutalities of war as the expression of an irrepressible human instinct. These writers subscribe more or less openly to the point of view of Ernest Jones in *Essays in Applied Psychoanalysis* in that their characters (or some of them) are "war lovers" and in the implication that war has an importance to human beings other than as a means of national policy:

Four repressed instincts play a cardinal part in all war: the passions for cruelty, destruction, lust, and loot. It is popularly held that the manifestations of these are incidental to War, and not inherent in it; that they are regrettable, though perhaps unavoidable, complications which should be reduced to a minimum. But it is found in practise that where one of these passions is suppressed another flames out the more to take its place; one army may rape where another loots.[5]

In the other category are writers like Shaw, Wouk, and Styron who imply, through the words and attitudes of their protagonists, that war is an aberration of human conduct and that civilized men are not drawn inexorably to indulge in it.

Some of the soldiers in these works, like Croft in *The Naked and the Dead* (1948), either overtly or implicitly find that war precipitates their latent killer instinct and offers them the chance to express what is presumably a permanent aspect of human nature. More important, the mood of all of these novels—stated more openly in *A Walk in the Sun* but implicit in the others—is that war had become interminable. In novels like *The Caine Mutiny* (1951), *Guard of Honor* (1948), and *The Young Lions* (1948) the soldiers look forward to the war being brought to a close by the defeat of the enemy; in the works of Mailer and Brown they look forward only to campaign after campaign until they are all destroyed. As a result the soldiers in these works, instead of having the unified outlook of the characters in the works of those authors who see war as a passing phenomenon, tend to be sharply divided into war lovers and pacifists. In *From Here to Eternity* (1951) Warden's cheerful cynicism is contrasted with Prewitt's Quakerish determination not to inflict unnecessary harm on anyone; in *The Naked and the Dead* Croft's positive delight in combat contrasts with Martinez's agonizing over the sinfulness of killing. In the novels of World War I the concept of the "war lover" would occasionally crop up; for example, the priest in *A Farewell to Arms* (1929), who identified himself with the peasants and their outlook, said, "[There] are people who would make war. In this country there are many like that."[6] More frequently the source of the war was associated with political or diplomatic issues. The most significant trend among the World War II novelists, which culminated in the novels of the absurd, was to recognize that war was not a passing phenomenon and to make explicit the element of individual responsibility in facing the problem of violence.

In some cases the World War II novels are marred by what appears to be a meretricious or oversimplified interpretation of the events of the war. The chapter headings of Herman Wouk's *The Caine Mutiny* ("Midshipman Keith," "Midshipman Keith in Trouble," etc.) suggest that the novel is actually an upgrading of the Hardy Boys tradition in which a clean-cut intelligent, well-meaning young chap gets involved in a nasty scrape but comes out all right in the end. The implication at least is that the novelist hastened to capitalize on wartime experience and in the process fell back on established formulas for successful popular writing. This contention is borne out by Greenwald's surprising drunken exoneration of Queeg at the end of *The Caine Mutiny*. After deriving the sensational benefits of pillorying the regular navy, Wouk evades any suggestion of anarchism by reaffirming the rightness of American institutions. A somewhat similar view can be taken of Irwin Shaw's purpose in *The Young Lions* with its crudely symbolic names (Christian, Michael, Noah, Green) and of Thomas Heggen's *Mister Roberts* (1946) which, with Roberts's warlike fervor toned down, saw long and successful service as a Broadway comedy.

These works come very close to the category described by Albert Van Nostrand as the "normal" or factory-produced novel: bulky; sensational in tone; reflecting "timely attitudes" toward "emotional disturbance, sexual difficulties and racial problems"; they are usually "brutally honest"—the saga of a group of private citizens assembled for military training and gradually built into a fighting unit, "imbued with camaraderie," who "test themselves in contact with the enemy at terrible cost." The popularity of these works after 1945 arose largely because a ready-made audience of several million ex-servicemen existed who wanted to read about themselves, because Berlin and Korea maintained popular interest in military affairs, and because the war novel lent itself to wide-screen extravaganza filming at a time when the movie industry was trying to combat the rising threat of television.[7]

Those novelists who attempted to see the war in philosophic terms usually diluted the impact that fiction based on firsthand experience of war could have for a civilian audience without achieving a deeper significance in their interpretation of those events. Cozzens's effort to make the reader appreciate the multiplicity of accidents that can plague a commander becomes over-long, a "tedious argument of insidious intent," while the continuously shifting viewpoint renders the story inchoate and baffles the reader. Mailer, on the other hand, muddies his limpid appreciation of the enlisted man in action by dropping wads of political discourse into his narrative. One can contrast Mailer's approach with that of James Jones who, although he is uncertain in his treatment of the officers in *From Here to Eternity*, does not make the mistake of trying to philosophize from the viewpoint of the academy graduate. He may suggest that the professional officers have peculiar sexual diversions and that they are narrow-minded to the point of obsession, but he makes his work revolve around that which he knows best—the life of a private infantry soldier.

The mocking vision of the soldier was manifested to a considerable extent in the novels of the First World War whose authors had experienced horror on so massive a scale that they were faced with the alternatives of laughter or numb withdrawal, and it was to become fundamental to the war novels of the late fifties; but the novels of World War II are more often characterized by a sober belief that if the team performs well and the coach calls the right plays, all will be well with humanity.

It is exactly this level-headed realism, coupled with a natural tendency to emphasize the sensational aspects of warfare, that has aroused a considerable body of adverse comment on these novels. As early as 1944 Joseph Remenyi voiced what was to become a general criticism of the novels of World War II: "They are sensational, but often boring; the writers of personal narratives are inclined to be garrulous or champions of 'thrillers.' "[8] Malcolm Cowley says that while they are technically more competent than the novels of World War I, they lack any examples of outstanding literary merit: "They form a tableland, not a chain of mountains."[9] Leslie Fiedler observes: "All the novels about the Second World War could never convince an intelligent observer from Betelgeuse that such an event had ever occurred; for they clearly represent the reaction of sensitive young men to a conflict they had read about during their high-school days."[10] John Aldridge complains that "it is as if [these novels] had been written too easily and their authors had had too painless an apprenticeship."[11] In all these comments one senses a typical American desire for either originality of plot or sensational statistics. Since war does not change in its fundamental characteristics (although the authors' perception of it might), and since the percentages of casualties in World War II were far lower than in World War I, these critics were bound to be deceived in their expectations. They did not perceive that the balanced outlook of some World War II authors would lead to a new assessment of the place of warfare in society.

Finally there is the well-founded charge, which could probably be leveled at the novelists of any war, that too many novels are restricted to a bald and utltimately boring realism: "This is the way it was, the author says. He was there and cannot be contradicted. . . . The urgency to explain 'the way it really was' . . . can dismiss cause and effect in favor of merely how it happened."[12] In many ways this aspect of the war novel is part of the tendency described by Philip Rahv for the American writer to depend too heavily on experience, as opposed to psychological interpretation, as the basis of his work[13]—a tendency that would naturally be aggravated in a wartime situation where many inexperienced writers would hasten to capitalize on a body of sensational experience.

If one recognizes the validity of these comments, it is also necessary to assess the reasons for the relative mediocrity of the World War II novels. William Phillips has claimed: "After the thirties writing took to greater realism in style and theme, to smaller subjects, to more recognizable worlds."[14] The tendency to seek mundane answers to the nation's problems was not peculiar to the war novel. In any case, if World War II was less disastrous than World War I in terms of American ideals, it was also less capable of dramatiziation in intensely personal terms. Early in the war Amy Loveman said, "The war remains for most of us an amorphous drama, impossible to realize in the agony of the individual, as we realized it in 1914 from the letters of a Victor Chapman or the correspondence of a Philip Gibbs."[15] This was largely because in World War II standardized military procedures had replaced the unorthodox, free-lance attitudes and roles of the men in the Norton-Harjes and Red Cross Ambulance Service. Commings walking the midnight road to La Ferté with his bedroll on his shoulder and the eighteen-year-old Hemingway seizing his moment of Italian heroism are unforgettable figures, but to Fiedler's observer from Betelgeuse Norman Mailer and James Jones must have been indistinguishable from thousands of other GIs as they trudged ashore in the Pacific.

Also, where a collection of highly articulate individuals saw World War I in the comparatively restricted arena of Western Europe, America's legion of identical units fought World War II in every part of the globe. The attention of both writers and audience was therefore divided from the outset; some saw and wrote about the war in the Pacific while others dealt with the European Theatre of Operations.[16] It was almost impossible for one man to have a synoptic view of the war. Furthermore, the nature of the war itself tended to reduce its dramatic value insofar as drama derives from controversy. As Cowley has said, the novelists of World

War II do not presume to judge the war largely because they were able to appreciate its objectives.[17] World War I was a long and bloody stalemate; in World War II the machine functioned, victories were clear-cut, the team rolled forward.

The complexity of the operations in the Second World War also brought home to the new generation of writers the increasing complexity of life in general. Referring to the works of Hemingway and Cummings, Aldridge says, "In each case, the emphasis was on the individual rather than the mass, the simple and concrete rather than the complex and ideological. . . . What Dos Passos saw in terms of the experience of three men, these writers see in terms of whole armies, whole societies."[18] This is the consideration that gave Norman Mailer pause in writing *The Naked and the Dead;* it is written in "the tone of a man whose capacity for political indignation is inhibited by a keen sense of the world as a very complicated place."[19] The cautiousness of the novelist in World War II was part of a growing political maturity.

Ultimately, however, the novelists' real difficulty in dramatizing World War II derived from the effect that World War I had had on the popular concepts of duty and heroism. "The notions of glory, honor, and courage lose all meaning when in the West men, still nominally Christian, come to believe that the worst thing of all is to die—when, for the first time in a thousand years, it is possible to admit that no cause is worth dying for."[20] Perhaps in the United States this loss of the sense of the heroic quality of combat was not completely assimilated until the nation had experienced a full-scale commitment to a foreign war, but the novels of World War II illustrate the increasing awareness of the problem. The writers are faced time and again with a fundamental dilemma; the novel that lacks a hero or heroic action tends to be mediocre and incohesive, and yet the traditional patterns of heroic conduct usually end in meaningless destruction. One sees this point illustrated in the film version of *The Bridge on the River Kwai* (1954). Shears's conduct follows a familiar pattern: he is the pragmatic American civilian in conflict with the martinets. As such he is no hero; yet when he is stimulated to heroic action by the events of the raid, he is killed uselessly along with everyone else. Perhaps the prime significance of the World War II novels written by American authors was that they allowed the writers to work out the conflict between native pragmatism and the heroic tradition. In this sense they represent the basis for the movement toward the absurd that occurred later in the decade.

11. KOREA

Although the end of World War II found the United States rather more conscious of its permanent role in world affairs than it had been after World War I, the country proceeded to demobilize its armed forces with customary rapidity. The idea that forces in being would become a permanent part of the American state was not yet widely accepted, although American foreign policy divested itself of all traits of isolationism for the first time in the nation's history—especially after 1947 when the Russians exploded their first nuclear device. The Americans permitted their conventional military forces to atrophy partly because of an overwhelming public demand for a return to peace time conditions; this atrophy was a reflection both of the universal confusion over the significance of the atomic bomb in world strategy and of the American tendency to see international problems as being susceptible to economic solutions. Although by early 1950 voices were being raised in protest against "the present strategic position . . . founded on a misplaced faith in nuclear weapons and strategic bombing,"[1] as the Korean War opened, the United States found itself with a largely dismantled military organization, a population just beginning to enjoy the fruits of peace and therefore reluctant to go back to war, and a strategy at once committed to the concept of all-out war and yet uncertain as to the real function of its prime weapon.

The fact that the United States was restrained from using nuclear weapons in Korea for political reasons was particularly demoralizing to a country whose prime article of tactical doctrine has always been that massive expenditure on firepower is preferable to loss of life, but even more debilitating was the reintroduction of the draft to fill the ranks of the armed forces. It has been noted that in the fiction of World War II the draft is rarely if ever a point of contention. However, it is also true that the "separate peace" motif so common in World War I novels barely appears in the novels of World War II. The implication is that the World War I soldiers, having volunteered or at least having been imbued with a spirit of idealism after they had been drafted, felt that they had thereby retained the right to withdraw from the conflict under certain circumstances. This feeling did not appear among the World War II combatants because they were less idealistic and because they had been conscripted. Eddie Slovik, the first man in eighty years to be "shot to death with musketry" in the United States Army for desertion in the face of the enemy, does not rail against his conscription as a violation of his right to decide whether or not he will serve in the armed forces of his country. To him the draft is only another of the inexorable forces conspiring to his downfall.

In the Korean War conscription was a particularly bitter pill to those who were called, even though there was relatively little public protest against it. Because Korea came fairly soon after World War II, the American populace accepted the drafting of a few hundred thousand troops to fight in a foreign war rather passively, although the high capture rate and the success of the Communist brainwashing program were manifestations of an underlying resentment on the part of the troops that were forced to serve in the field while the people at home went on enjoying life. It is this type of selfish rather than idealistic resentment that characterizes the fiction of the Korean War. In both William Styron's *The Long March* (1953) and James Michener's *The Bridges at Toko-ri* (1953) the protagonists are men who served in World War II and are sullenly opposed to what they consider to be an unjust demand made on them when they were beginning to enjoy life for the first time. Both Al Mannix and Harry Brubaker agonize over the manner in which they are being deprived of the comfort of their homes; Lieutenant Culver "felt weirdly as if he had fallen asleep in some barracks in 1945 and had awakened in a half-dozen years or so to find that the intervening freedom, growth, and serenity had been only a glorious if somewhat prolonged dream."[2]

These men found themselves trapped by the system in that they could not quit while they saw others going on. To make things worse, as Brubaker insists in *The Bridges at Toko-ri,* no one in America knows what Korea is about, or cares. Korea, then, marks a turning point in the American citizen's attitude toward war. From this point onward the individual thinks of himself first and is immune to appeals to his idealism or patriotism—on the grounds that war seems likely to be a continuing factor in human affairs as long as men consent to serve, that the nation's wars never seem to achieve their goals, and most of all that fighting is a dangerous occupation. By the time the United States became fully involved in Viet Nam, the opposition to conscription had become general and voluble despite a much longer propaganda campaign in favor of American intervention in that country. But the antiwar demonstrations and draft-card burnings in the sixties are not manifestations of the old conscientious objector spirit; they are not humanitarian in the largest sense. Rather they are related to Yossarian's argument in reply to the standard question, Suppose everyone felt that way about military service? " 'Then I'd certainly be a damned fool to feel any other way, wouldn't I?' "[3] A primordial instinct for self-preservation replaced to a large extent the pure idealism which had motivated the conscientious objectors of World War I.

The literature of the Korean War records the beginning of a new concept of pacifism based on a purely realistic, self-centered attitude on the part of those representatives of the civilian population that were drafted into service; it also reaffirms the existence of the ascetic, rather fascistic devotion to militarism of the professional soldier. In *The Professional Soldier* (1960) Morris Janowitz concludes that under the prolonged tensions of the cold war it is possible for a democracy to be transformed into a "garrison state" in which the military comes to have a disproportionate significance and authority. Janowitz expresses a hope that the "constabulary force" concept will allow the professional soldier to retain the traditional fighting motivations of honor and national security while remaining subordinate to the civilian authority.[4] In the novels about the Korean War, the first in which the constabulary force was employed, this hope is not fully rewarded. Colonel Templeton in *The Long March* is described as a man in whom "all emotions—all smiles, all anger—emanated from a priestlike fervour, throbbing inwardly with the cadence of parades and booted footfalls."[5] Admiral Tarrant in *The Bridges at Toko-ri* goes even further when he voices the opinion that America is involved in "an unending war of many generations."[6] The civilians have not yet realized the fact that real peace is a fantasy, and Tarrant envisions the task of the regular officer as both standing on guard against the nation's enemies and striving to awaken the civilian population to the omnipresent danger.

A similar attitude is attributed to a career captain in the marines in Pat Frank's *Hold Back the Night* (1952). This novel, based on the First Marine Division's retreat from the Yalu to Hamhung, deals with three days in the life of one company that has been assigned the task of covering the withdrawal and is decimated in the process. Captain MacKenzie, the company commander, sees soldiering as a fine, desirable, and necessary profession in existing world circumstances. Another officer—who is captured by the Chinese and expresses doubts about the purpose of the war, UN cooperation, and President Truman—is described as having "a dark area in his mind." MacKenzie is perfectly attuned to the military organization; he realizes that "in this exclusive brotherhood, he was still a neophyte. . . . He hoped, one day, to be a full member."[7]

The fiction of the Korean War revealed a marked division in the American attitude toward warfare and the military establishment. That part of the civilian population that was called to serve in the armed forces tended to be bitterly resentful of the fact. Since conscription affected only a small minority of the people, those who were called were made even more conscious of the discriminatory aspects of the system, and this disgruntlement caused them to question the purpose and value of the nation's war aims. Yet the prospect of the United States being involved in fairly serious wars every few years, which was so distasteful to the civilian mind, provided the basis for increasing self-confidence on the part of the military. To them Korea provided substance for the argument that traditional American military policy in regard to the status of the professional soldier would have to be permanently altered for the first time in 175 years.

12. BLURRING OF DISTINCTION BETWEEN CIVILIAN AND MILITARY ORGANIZATIONS

In the period from 1945 to 1960 the distinction between military and civilian establishments and modes of operation became increasingly blurred, until it practically ceased to exist. This blurring was a result of three main factors: the military's long campaign to achieve a significant role in American life, the aftermath of World War II, and the advent of the cold war. The process that took place in this period was not one of military domination of civilian affairs, as feared by President Eisenhower; rather it was the assumption by the military of a permanent (if secondary) role in the affairs of state and, on the part of the civilians, a growing comprehension of military affairs and greater expertise in the field of strategy. The traditional diastole and systole of the American military establishment was arrested for the first time in the nation's history as the logic of the cold war obliged the armed forces to adopt new postures and new configurations and as the same logic bred a new degree of strategic understanding and competence in the civilian administrators. The fundamental doctrine of civilian domination of the military was retained and even strengthened in this period, but the modes of operation of the civil and military organizations became practically interchangeable, while the characteristic ethos of the professional soldier was eroded and modified under the pressures of the nuclear age.

The dismissal of MacArthur in a sense marked the end of the domination of the services by the old-style officer—who was strictly

militaristic in his outlook, rather puritanical in his concept of
civilian life, and entirely apolitical in his thinking—and the advent
of a new type of officer better equipped to work interchangeably
with the civilian administration. In this, as in some other areas,
the cold war tended to fuse the functions of civilian and military
personnel which had hitherto been sharply differentiated.

The necessity for the military to think in terms of diplomatic
and political possibilities became increasingly evident after Hiroshima. Before World War II the military capabilities of individual
nations tended to be fairly stable while alliances changed; the
nation's security therefore rested to a large extent on the skill and
foresight of the diplomatic corps. After 1945 alliances tended to be
fixed while military power fluctuated rapidly.[1] "The traditional
distinctions of diplomacy—between belligerents and neutrals, between external and internal affairs, between a state of war and a
state of peace—are slowly losing their meaning."[2] In a situation
where diplomacy lost its preeminence over the military organization, the function of the diplomat had to be replaced partly by that
of the politician and the social scientist and partly by the military
themselves. The new conditions of the cold war called for officers
whose function was primarily that of negotiator rather than commander, just as they eventually called for a new standard of knowledge and expertise in military affairs on the part of politicians and
civil servants.

The situation which was to culminate in the Kennedy-
McNamara defense policies had been foreseen by Vannevar Bush
in 1946 when he said that the development and strategic doctrine
governing the use of new weapons must become a continuing process and there must be a greater probability of officers with primarily scientific training rising to positions of influence in the
armed forces.[3] The process he forecast also enhanced the tendency
for military personnel to become indistinguishable from civilians.
The cold war necessitated a constant state of readiness, and it became clear that the academies could not supply the necessary number of officers. More and more officers from nonmilitary backgrounds and with highly specialized technical training—which
tended to make them disregard the importance of tradition and
ritual codes of conduct—were drafted or enlisted, thereby diluting
the values and motivations traditionally ascribed to the professional
soldier.

Morris Janowitz points out that the military in any modern
industrial society tend to become "civilianized" rather than the
civilians becoming militarized. This situation is a natural result of
the necessity for the military to adopt modern management techniques and organizations and to maintain closer liaison with industry and politics.[4] In the United States the trend away from the

isolation of the military establishment was accentuated by the genesis and development of techniques of operations research during and after World War II—techniques based essentially on a marriage of scientists and economists in order to solve technological problems as they arose and to fit the solutions into the nation's strategic framework.

Since the operations researchers were primarily civilians and because the subject of war had become so complex and subtle that it attracted the interest of the nation's best scholars, one of the most significant results of the postwar period was that the military began to defer to the scientists in questions of strategy, military policy, and even tactics. The defining and assessment of such esoteric strategic nuances as the "barely nuclear war," the "exemplary counterforce attack," and the "slow-motion counterforce war"[5] called for the attention of the best minds in the nation, regardless of whether those minds belonged to military or civilian personnel. The situation is summed up by William R. Kintner in an essay entitled "Political Requirements for United States Strategy":

The next issue . . . is the downgrading of professional military people in the determination of the national strategy. I would say that now they are about at the third or fourth level on the totem pole when it comes to making up choices [involving weapons, levels of forces, employment of troops in a given situation]. I would further contend it is mostly their own fault. Service parochialism still prevents the military from forming a genuine consensus as to the nature of the strategic problems confronting them. Another aspect of the problem, however, is the advent of the distinguished civilian analysts . . . who have gained tremendous influence for one simple reason. They have done their homework on the complicated and difficult issues of defense far better than many of the professional military have.[6]

Dr. Henry Kissinger is an excellent example of the point Kintner is making.

As this process of mutation and subordination was taking place in the realms of research and strategy, even the primary role of the soldier was becoming obliterated in a situation where wars were either too dangerous to actually be fought or too small to require the services of other than a handful of specialists; the traditional military officer—the "generalist" skilled in the command of troops in battle—was caught between the technician on the one hand and the guerrilla on the other.[7]

The tendency for military personnel to become indistinguishable from civilians was reflected even in such minor matters as the evolution of armed forces' wearing apparel after 1939. Traditionally military uniforms were designed to differentiate the wearer from the civilian masses. Even as late as 1939 American troops wore the high-collared tunic and stiff forage cap that had devolved from the formal uniforms of the nineteenth century. Then during World War II came the "Eisenhower" jacket—a variation on standard golfing apparel—and battle dress that was a modification of the lumberjack's heavy woolen shirt. At the same time aircrew personnel began wearing baseball caps and coveralls. After 1945 the Russians and then the Americans altered the military uniform until, in the fifties, it became more or less a sack suit with brass buttons. The process of amalgamation has continued steadily since that time. When President Nixon met President Thieu at Okinawa early in 1969, it was observed that some of Nixon's civilian aides "came arrayed in semimilitary jackets with epaulets on the shoulders, the Presidential seal above the right breast pocket, and the wearer's name (H. Kissinger, for example) stenciled on the left."[8]

In the realm of fiction the blurring of the distinction between soldier and civilian resulted in three different reactions. Some writers tried to satisfy the enduring demand for heroic literature by creating new avatars for the hero; others reworked the vein of World War II experience as melodrama; and a third group attempted to deal realistically with the image of the military and the civilians as a corporate entity.

Even in an era when the professional soldier had come increasingly to resemble a corporation vice-president, the demand for tales of heroic action persisted. Henry Brandon has said that John F. Kennedy's fascination with the idea of an American guerrilla force (i.e., the Green Berets) was "part of the search for ways to exalt the role of the individual, the heroic man, in a world made too dangerous by the threat of nuclear war."[9] Similarly, it has been observed that "Norman Mailer . . . continues his search for a twentieth-century hero."[10] It would be difficult to select two men more representative of America in the early sixties than Mailer and Kennedy; that they should both remain preoccupied with the question of heroic action in the midst of absurdity seems indicative of a tendency among Americans as a whole.

As a result of this continuing public desire, the hero appeared in some surprising avatars after World War II. The most important of these was the phenomenon that began with Mickey Spillane's publication of I, the Jury in 1947. The formula of the crime or detective novel involving a tough, smooth-talking hero had been established as far back as 1930 in the works of Dashiell Hammett and Raymond Chandler. In fact the entire Spillane formula—the specially equipped car, the arsenal of weapons, the beautiful female consort—had been represented in the film version of The Big Sleep (1939), with Humphrey Bogart playing the part of the indestructible hero. Yet Chandler's work met with only modest success. On the other hand, in 1947 Spillane's first novel sold 5 million copies, as did his successive reworkings of the theme in 1950 and 1951. At about the same time Ian Fleming marketed a similar formula in England with equal success. In the course of fifteen years Fleming and Spillane together sold over 80 million copies of their novels.

John McCormick's comment that "[the bestseller] is the point at which literature and sociology unfortunately coincide"[11] suggests that these novels responded to a deeply felt public desire. In this sense one can assume that Fleming and Spillane were satisfying a widespread demand for a fictional hero. There is very little critical comment on Spillane's work,[12] but numerous critics have assessed that of Fleming and are almost unanimous in pinpointing the heroic metamorphosis. Even critics like George Grella—who admit that Fleming's work lacks the subtlety and plausibility of Chandler, Graham Greene, or Eric Ambler and that James Bond is "stupid" —still claim that the key to his popularity lies in the fact that these novels are not thrillers but "historic epic and romance, based on the stuff of myth and legend."[13] That this is no casual opinion is shown by the careful working out of the analogies between Bond and the heroes of antiquity.[14]

During this same period other American writers were reworking World War II experiences from the traditional point of view— i.e., that point of view which sees warfare and the military establishment as a significant and isolated part of the national life. In their novels the war tends to become a framework rather than a theme: the events of the war are no longer valuable as original experiences in themselves, but the war itself and the military organization still serve as familiar frames of reference for drama or comedy. The treatment of wartime events becomes ritualized, an aspect that is even more noticeable in the films and television series based on World War II. In the comedies the soldiers are carefree, good-natured scoundrels and in the melodramas they are humble, brave, and generous. The war story in this case has become as stylized as the Western; the characters, no longer able to enthrall the audience with straight narrative about wartime adventures, turn to acting out various aspects of the American mythos.

Among the war novels John Hersey's *The War Lover* (1959) is a prime example of this tendency. Although Hersey was not a combatant like Wouk, Mailer, or Jones, his service as a war correspondent in the Pacific and in Europe gave him sufficient exposure to combat that, fourteen years after the war ended, he was able to write what commonly passes for a war novel. In itself *The War Lover* is a fairly competent account of the life of a bomber crew stationed in England during World War II. The details are all true to life; the story line is neatly worked out and quite intriguing. For all the technical competence displayed by the author, however, the novel lacks something of the immediacy and impact of those works written in the first flush of wartime experience. One is dimly conscious of the fact that the author has taken the concept of the "war lover" and built a novel around it, thereby producing quite a different effect from a story written by a man who was actually in combat. On the other hand, Hersey's use of the war novel for moralizing purposes also places him outside the group of novelists who, although lacking in combat experience, still treated the theme objectively.

Hersey's traditional point of view is revealed in the primary theme (war is wicked and unpleasant), in the subsidiary theme (in modern war most of the combatants have lost the sense of personal involvement), and in the neat denouement (the war lover, Buzz Marrow, realizes the hopelessness of his ways and sinks with his plane while Bo Boman, the open-minded all-American boy, turns out to be a conventional hero and is reunited with the girl). *The War Lover* does not really qualify as a novel of protest because Marrow is regarded as something of a freak; the war lovers are not seen to be a predominant group in society, and their vagaries are susceptible to control by the more rational actions of their comrades. Rather, the novel is an exploitation of the war as a framework for the ritual development of a familiar American theme.

In some cases, like Kurt Vonnegut's *Player Piano* (1952), the blurring of the distinction between soldier and civilian is treated as a sardonic vision of the future. *Player Piano* is not a war novel by any means, but it does contain an amusing scene on board a train in which a recruiting sergeant accompanying a group of trainees to their destination regales the young soldiers with tales of his combat experiences. His story opens conventionally enough: "Jesus, there we was and there they was, . . . a hog-back, with the bastards dug in deep on the reverse slope." But it soon transpires that the old sergeant and his men had no intention of engaging the enemy personally. Their anxieties derived from the fact that the generator that supplied power for the platoon's arsenal of automated weapons had been knocked out. At the crucial moment a new generator is found, the computerized weapons take over the battle, and, as the sergeant explains, "That's how I got the Silver Star."[15]

The more characteristic novels of the period from 1953 to 1963 are those like Philip Wylie's *Tomorrow!* (1954), Eugene Burdick and Harvey Wheeler's *Fail-Safe* (1962), and Fletcher Knebel and Charles W. Bailey's *Seven Days in May* (1962); these attempt to treat warfare and the military establishment in terms of the conditions of the nuclear age. None of these novels is of extraordinary literary merit. They tend to be slick and highly readable examples of the American ability to mass-produce and package an idea for popular consumption, but they do serve to illustrate the contention that the role of the military officer in America has undergone a qualitative change and has assumed a secondary position in the affairs of the nation.

In all these works preeminence is given to politicians and scientists rather than to military officers in times of crisis. In *Tomorrow!* the focus is on the civil defense organizations of two neighboring midwestern cities, one of which prepares for nuclear attack and the other does not. Perhaps the greatest merit of *Tomorrow!* is that it evokes perfectly the fear and anxiety-ridden mentality of America in the early fifties when terror of the bomb was predominant in everyone's mind. Unfortunately Wylie attributes the national hysteria to the military as well as the civilian population. When he refers to the military, his portrait of the professional officer is an odd one; he pictures officers in a time of crisis abandoning tasks to which they have been assigned in favor of manning planes to engage the enemy personally. The commanding general of the region delays giving the red alert for perfectly legitimate reasons and then shoots himself when he begins to realize the magnitude of the disaster, instead of carrying on with whatever could be done to restore the situation.

In both *Fail-Safe* and *Seven Days in May* the problems that arise are no longer thought of as being capable of solution by force of arms. No longer does the United States Cavalry charge figuratively to the rescue. Instead every effort is made to reach a negotiated settlement where possible, with the military officers participating as members of the negotiating team. The emphasis is on the "logic of politics" rather than the logic of force.

In his book on President Kennedy, Theodore Sorensen explains how the President came to downgrade the value of the militarist approach to international problems, especially after the Bay of Pigs episode. Sorensen describes the first reaction to the Cuban missile situation as the traditional Clausewitz-type approach in which the military and some civilian advisers urged an invasion of Cuba. He also describes the manner in which Kennedy and his aides carefully worked out a detailed solution to the problem—a solution that necessarily forebade the use of military force in the first instance.[16]

This same outlook shapes the events of *Fail-Safe* and *Seven Days in May*. In *Fail-Safe* a group of six bombers proceeds on a bombing mission over Moscow due to a mechanical failure in the computerized control system at SAC headquarters:[17] in *Seven Days in May* a group of senior American officers plot to take over the government of the United States in order to prevent the country from ratifying a disarmament treaty. In both novels an officer recommends traditional hard-line military action—by preparing for all-out war in one case and by arresting the chiefs of staff in the other. In both cases the prime task of the President is to prevent such precipitate action while working out a solution to the problem in terms of what is politically possible.

Although these novels deal with war or the threat of war, the military play a secondary role. The problem of war at this point has essentially become one that must be negotiated primarily by civilians, both because their knowledge of the subject is far wider than that of the military and because their approach is the only one holding some promise of success.

These novels also illustrate the writers' new conception of the role and character of the military officer. The distinction between the old-style and the new-style officer is reflected both in the motivation and the training. The old-style officer, who had probably served in World War II, is still the activist—highly trained in his own field, completely apolitical, deriving his motivation from the tradition of the service and his satisfaction from a sense of comradeship and the knowledge of his own competence. The new-style officer (like General Black in *Fail-Safe* or General Scott in *Seven Days in May*) remains physically brave and professionally competent but is also oriented to think in terms of the political consequences of his actions and to act as a partner in the civil-military organization.

More important, these officers function efficiently without requiring the soldier's sense of comradeship and without being emotionally involved in their tasks. It was the prospect of this sort of existence that made Melville Goodwin wish he had been buried with his dead comrades along the Rhine. He, like Colonel Casey in *Seven Days in May* and Colonel Grady in *Fail-Safe*, is an old-style officer and a member of a vanishing breed. This point is especially emphasized in *Fail-Safe* where the three-man crew of one American bomber is composed of Colonel Grady and two younger officers. The younger officers are mere technicians—interchangeable parts of a vast machine in which

the crew almost never talk except over the intercom; in fact, the crew members make very little small talk with one another, partly because their training has discouraged it, and partly because they are seldom close friends.

It had recently become SAC policy to circulate crew members at random among planes. The objective was to get identical performance from all men so that they acted as identical units of a class rather than as individual personalities. Given the cost and the speed and the importance of a Vindicator, no one wanted to count on camaraderie or crew morale for a mission to be successful.[18]

But Grady is the emotional descendant of Henry Fleming and Robert E. Lee Prewitt. There is no real difference between the satisfaction that Prewitt derives from his skill as a rifleman and Grady's joy in flying the last of the manned bombers. As Grady brings the big aircraft screaming in over the Russian landscape at 1,500 miles an hour and knows that his own courage and intellect have brought him within striking distance of the enemy, he cannot restrain himself from shouting joyfully into the intercom, "We're making like a fat-assed bird." But the only response is a cautious glance from the navigator and defense operator; after all, "there was no reason under current procedures why he had to talk to the other two men in the plane at all."[19] Under these conditions it is almost impossible for the professional soldier to be the hero of a significant literary work.

In these novels the civilians display a new attitude toward warfare and the military establishment. Warfare tends to be seen as a disaster, but one which may possibly be kept within bounds if the military are prevented from taking over the situation. In *Tomorrow!* the Russians are annihilated by a primitive superbomb after the civil defense organization has managed to salvage a considerable part of the American population and economy; in *Fail-Safe* the President averts war by working out a quid pro quo with Premier Kruschev. After two American bombers have accidentally devastated Moscow, the President orders an American bomber to destroy New York. In both cases the problem is solved by corporate action between the civilians and the military, with the military playing a definitely secondary role in the actual conduct of the hostilities. General Black in *Fail-Safe* is continuously present at the Cabinet meeting during which the President negotiates his agreement with Premier Kruschev, like a junior vice-president in charge of dropping the bomb. As in *Seven Days in May,* the logic of politics and the corporate decision are the criteria by which what would formerly have been military problems are now resolved.

It cannot be argued that the new directions taken by the war novel in the fifties are due solely to a lack of wartime experience. Since World War II, defense expenditures and the military establishment have reached an unprecedented size and the nation has engaged in an impressive array of hot wars and armed interventions—Korea, Laos, the Dominican Republic, Viet Nam. Two significant factors seem to control the output of war fiction during this period: (1) the line of demarcation between the roles of the civilian and military elements has become less and less distinct (for example, the CIA became increasingly militant, while vast numbers of soldiers were occupied in pacification and resettlement work in places like Viet Nam), and (2) the scope of the wars has not been great enough to generate the sort of national experience that underlies any important body of literature. Even Viet Nam cannot compare in the universality of its experience with World Wars I and II. The 600,000 troops engaged there were a pittance compared to the 15 million Americans who were in uniform in World War II; the 36,000 dead in the first four years of action were only one quarter of the number of people killed on American highways in the same period. The war was expensive, but so were the space program and the problem of the cities. In other words, these post-Korean wars have not outweighed the other problems that have faced the nation in the last twenty years.

The real problem in this period was the cold war—specifically the question of national defense against nuclear attack. But this problem was met by vast expenditures of cash in the manner of a huge corporation, on the one hand, and by the development of an army of technicians like Vonnegut's sergeant, on the other. Neither of these elements was capable of effective dramatization, a fact which resulted in the rather peripheral quality of the novels that attempt to deal in a traditional manner with the military establishment in this period.

13. THE ABSURD

War novel publication in the United States followed an interesting pattern in the period from 1944 to 1962. Approximately 250 novels dealing with the events of World War II had been published by the late fifties.[1] Of these the greatest number had been written between 1944 and 1952; thereafter publication became sporadic. Furthermore, in these novels war is still treated in fairly conventional terms as a vastly impressive experience; the author's primary object is not usually to express a sense of revulsion.

Between 1957 and 1962 the publication of a small but important group of novels heralded a new approach to war literature on the part of American writers. Mark Harris's *Something about a Soldier* (1957), Joseph Heller's *Catch-22* (1961), Kurt Vonnegut's *Mother Night* (1962), and to a considerable extent James Jones's *The Thin Red Line* (1962) share the common characteristic of treating warfare in terms of the absurd. It is perhaps important to underline the fact that these novels form a quite clearly defined group. They were all published within a period of five years, and they appeared when publication of conventional records of wartime experiences had begun to taper off. Joseph Heller confirms that in his case at least this timing was no accident: "I put off writing my own [novel] for eight years because of them."[2] In this sense it is clear that *Catch-22* was influenced by the work of writers like Wouk and Mailer and yet is in quite a different category from their novels. The works of Harris, Heller, Vonnegut, and Jones share enough similarities in outlook and treatment to draw fairly strong comparisons between them.

The relationship between warfare and the literature of the absurd was by no means restricted to the United States, nor was it confined to the post-Korean period. If anything, it found its origin and greatest impetus in the horrors of World War I. Although the European nations had suffered greater losses in the First World War than had the Americans, the Americans were more deeply shocked, because of their initial idealism, than the Europeans by the events of the war. Thus the atmosphere of the absurd crept into war literature on both sides of the Atlantic in the period after

1918. In the midst of a series of humorous sketches of life in the trenches, for example, "L'interprète Aurelle" had asked,

Pourquoi . . . notre existence ne se partagerait-elle pas en trois états: le sommeil, la vie, forme secondaire de sommeil; et un troisième dont nous n'avons aucune idée et dans lequel nous nous réveillerons au sortir de ce songe absurde? Quand on rêve, on ne sait pas qu'on rêve; si cette vie est un cauchemar, nous ne le saurons qu'après sa fin. Alors, peut-être, nous retrouvant dans un monde familier, comprendrons-nous soudain que cette guerre, ces folies, nos souffrances ont été les fantômes terribles et vains d'une courte nuit de la vie véritable.[3]

In 1930 the publication in Czechoslovakia of Jaroslav Hasek's *The Good Soldier Schweik* established an early and enduring example of the absurd. These European works shared something of the tone and mood of Cummings's *The Enormous Room* (1922) in that they sought to satirize that aspect of war which appeared to transcend mere indignation.

The absurd suffered a certain setback during and immediately after World War II for a variety of reasons. In England there was an apparent unwillingness or inability to treat the war in other than conventional terms. V. S. Pritchett has observed: "After the Thirties, European novelists had nothing new to say about land battle as a subject. . . . In the Second World War an experience here or there might make its claim and even be well-done for the record, but the content was too predictable."[4] John McCormick claims that the British had exhausted their capacity for indignation in World War I; as a result, in the period after World War II "English war novelists as a group have written with a superficial command which stops at competence and evades the challenge of the theme."[5]

Furthermore, the absurd became inappropriate in writing of a war that many of the participants came to regard as a "just" war. Even a man like H. Stuart Hughes, who describes himself as "not a pacifist, but . . . a historian who finds very few wars worth fighting" (including the American Revolutionary War, the American Civil War, and World War I), still feels that World War II was worth fighting.[6] Whatever one's beliefs might have been regarding war in general, the extermination camps in Europe were an indisputable fact attesting the justness of the Allied effort in World War II.

In Germany too the sense of having fought with skill and courage against overwhelming odds produced an elegiac rather than a satirical note in many of the novels about the war. Works like Peter Bamm's *The Invisible Flag* (1956) and Theodore Plivier's *Stalingrad* (1957) share something of the tone of *All Quiet on the Western Front* (1929); the soldier serves bravely in a losing cause, perhaps regretting this disaster that has shattered his life but still powerfully motivated by a sense of duty and comradeship. One of the very best of these novels, Heinrich Böll's *The Train Was on Time* (1949), characteristically combines the fatalism of the protagonist with a surrealistic symbolism that evokes a sense of inevitable destruction.

In Russia writing about the war was complicated by a necessity for political orthodoxy, with the result that until Stalin's death the Russian war novel tended to be a variation on the "boy meets tractor" sagas designed to urge the workers to greater efforts under the Communist regime. After the death of Stalin there was a certain detente, and authors found themselves free to write honestly about the great actions on the eastern front.[7] Still the absurd did not manifest itself in these works, both because political freedom did not extend quite that far and because the writers were fully occupied with conventional treatments of the war.

Despite these reasons for treating the experiences of World War II in conventional terms, as the decade of the fifties advanced the satirical note once again crept into the war novels from both sides of the Atlantic. In Germany a particularly rich lode was formed by the publication of Helmut Kirst's *Forward Gunner Asch* (1956), Karl-Ludwig Opitz's *The General* (1956), and Friedrich Deich's *The Sanity Inspectors* (1957). Gunner Asch creates chaos in the well-regulated German army by a form of work-to-rule: e.g., the regulations state that each man is entitled to one hundred grams of meat per day; when it is Asch's turn to serve the meat in the men's kitchen, he stalls the entire operation by meticulously weighing each ration on a set of chemist's scales. The hero of *The Sanity Inspectors* is a psychiatrist whose assessment of the German war effort leads him to certify pilot trainees for admission to nursing homes where they will be safe until the war ends.

This same note of desperate satire pervades many of the war novels published in Europe in this period—including *The Legion of the Damned* by Sven Hassel (1957), Egon Hostovsky's *The Lonely Rebels* (1957), Ivan Bahrianyi's *The Hunters and the Hunted* (1955), and Pierre Boulle's *The Bridge on the River Kwai* (1954). The international scope of the movement is revealed by the fact that Hassel is a Dane who served in a German penal battalion, Hostovsky is a Czech, Bahrianyi is a Ukrainian in exile, and Boulle is a Frenchman.

The question then arises as to what stimulated this expression of the sense of the absurdity of war, of which the works of Harris, Heller, Vonnegut, and Jones form one segment. In the realm of the American war novel at least, it can be seen as the natural working out of an attitude that was implicit in the early novels of World War II. In those works the characters often had an ambivalent attitude toward warfare and the military establishment; they could be loyal to the unit and even to the objectives of this particular war but dismayed by the idea of war as a continuing influence in human affairs. As William Styron has said of his generation, "We were the most distrustful of power and the least nationalistic of any generation that America has produced. . . . Whatever its defects may have been, it has been this generation's interminable experience with ruthless power and the loony fanaticism of the military mind that by and large caused it to lend the most passionate support to the struggle to end war everywhere."[8]

The treatment of warfare in terms of the absurd derives also from the loss of a sense of the ennobling aspect of combat, an effect which had been growing in the public mind ever since the holocaust of World War I and was reinforced by events like the firebombing of Dresden and Hamburg in World War II. If during the earlier wars the public was only remotely aware of this aspect of war, the technology of the cold war made it universally apparent. Samuel P. Huntington claims that "American outrage at the war [in Viet Nam] . . . reflected less the war than it did the impact of television."[9] The romance of the soldier's art had depended partly on an element of mystery which was best cultivated in isolation from the public eye; but the elements of emotion and mystery vital to the concepts of militarism and hero worship cannot survive when the public is exposed to the spectacle of an American soldier burning down a grass hut with a Zippo lighter.

Finally the sense of the absurdity of further conflict derived from a national realization that none of the wars in which the nation had engaged had ultimately achieved their long-term purpose. Writing about the characteristics of modern war, Walter Millis said that Waterloo was the last battle that decided anything with finality in one day: "War was beginning to lose its one virtue —its power of decision."[10] Even extending the time element does not seem to compensate for the tendency of industrialized war to arrive at a different conclusion from that which was intended. The nation had seen the 1918 military victory disappear in the economic and political upheavals of the early 1920s, the defeat of the Axis in 1945 was apparently frittered away at Yalta and Potsdam, and the Korean War produced the costliest and least satisfying result of all. The nuclear age offered only the prospect of dying as uselessly as previous generations had died, and in much greater numbers. Under these conditions it is not surprising that the nation's writers should express an awareness of the absurdity of the situation and try to offer an alternative to the prospect of destruction.

The novels themselves represent a summing up and a response to the problem of warfare and the military establishment in the modern age. The superhuman society capable of engulfing the individual and churning him out as a mass-produced unit to fight in its wars had become increasingly a source of concern to the American novelists. In *Guard of Honor* (1948) James Gould Cozzens said, "The dismaying sense of it, perhaps the one common denominator in the various feelings of several million men caught up in a war, of steady, in the exact sense, preposterous, compulsion, oppressed the mind. It reversed accustomed order and reasoned expectation."[11]

Yet there apparently was nothing the individual could do about the reversal of "accustomed order and reasoned expectation"; the course of events was so overpowering that conformity was inevitable. The ball turret gunner in Randall Jarrell's poem says, "From my mother's sleep I fell into the State"; Captain Stein in *The Thin Red Line* sees warfare as part of "the great conspiracy of history"; Corporal Fife feels trapped by a force that is both anonymous and powerful—"trapped in every direction no matter where he turned, trapped by patriotic doctors, trapped by long-faced crewcut infantry Colonels who demanded the willingness to die, trapped by Japanese colonial ambitions, trapped by chic grinning S-1 officers secure in their right to ask only after other officers, trapped by his own government and its faceless nameless administrators."[12] In *Catch-22* these omnipotent forces pass into the realm of the weird and invisible; those who object to the way the system functions can be "disappeared," like Dunbar, or terrorized and imprisoned by remorseless military police operating under the all-powerful rubric of "Catch-22."

For Jacob Epp in *Something about a Soldier* the dilemma is even harsher. He has no experience of life, no knowledge of bureaucracy or corruption. His whole attitude toward warfare is theoretical and idealistic; furthermore, he is a Jew and feels the personal necessity of opposing Nazism. To him the dilemma consists of either having to fight, which is irrational and repugnant, or failing in his duty and being oppressed. Even the sardonic Welsh in *The Thin Red Line* is baffled by the forces that have conspired to make him fight: "All Welsh knew was that he was scared shitless, and at the same time was afflicted with a choking gorge of anger that any social coercion existed in the world which could force him to be here."[13] All these men share the overpowering realization that the real enemy is war itself.

In this context the novelists of the absurd set about destroying the myths that have contributed to the glorification of the profession of arms. In *Catch-22* the brash young officers who are sent into Yossarian's squadron as replacements are seen as simple-minded adolescents living in the belief that war is some sort of college prank. In contrast with this naiveté, the ruthlessness of Milo's character overpowers the familiar image of the endearing military scoundrel, just as James Jones's portrait of Private Doll in *The Thin Red Line* penetrates and exposes "that fiction beloved in all armies of the tough, scrounging, cynical soldier who collects whatever he can get his hands on."

In all these novels the soldier is shown to be cowardly, dishonest, self-seeking, and immoral—a point made clearer by the contrast between the characters of Prewitt in *From Here to Eternity* and Witt in *The Thin Red Line.* The young, intelligent, rather romantic soldier—who is also a capable artist—becomes a caricature of himself. Both Witt and Prewitt love the army and are competent soldiers, but in Witt the human elements have disappeared; he is practically an idiot, neither physically nor morally attractive. The shift in Jones's viewpoint is illustrated by the fact that Prewitt's individualism becomes Witt's perversity and Prewitt's loyalty to his private code of conduct becomes Witt's "goddamed, stupid Kentucky code."

The divergence in outlook between the war novelists of the absurd and writers of traditional war novels can be seen if one contrasts a book like James Fenimore Cooper's *The Spy* (1821) with Vonnegut's *Mother Night.* The story line in each case is almost identical—an American citizen risks his life and reputation in order to act as a spy in the camp of the enemy—but there the similarity ends. Cooper's spy ends his service to the revolutionary cause with a refusal of any form of reward from General Washington. He dies in the War of 1812, "as he had lived, devoted to his country, and a martyr to her liberties." Vonnegut's Howard W. Campbell, Jr., on the other hand, has the opportunity to discuss his reasons for becoming a spy with the American officer who had served as his contact during the war. They arrive at the gloomy conclusion that the only real reason for his actions is that, "generally speaking, espionage offers each spy an opportunity to go crazy in a way he finds irresistible." Cooper's spy lives to old age and dies a hero's death; Vonnegut's eventually commits suicide.

Doll and Dale in *The Thin Red Line,* Aarfy in *Catch-22,* and Toat in *Something about a Soldier* are all either completely insensitive to what they are doing or are motivated by the lowest human instincts. It has been noted that as far back as the Revolution, "in classic fashion, the military emphasized the evil in man, man's natural pride, acquisitiveness and avarice. For the American officer, the duality of good and evil in human nature made war inevitable."[14] The professional officers in the novels of the absurd respond accordingly, flogging their unwilling recruits into battle in a spirit of icy detachment.

The novelists of the absurd use the contrast between the strictly selfish and objective approach of the professional officers and the romanticism of the draftees to destroy the myth of comradeship or the bond of affection between officers and men. To Yossarian Colonel Cathcart represents the system and therefore is the real enemy. In *The Thin Red Line,* as each officer or NCO is promoted to command, a gush of paternal sentiment for his troops sweeps over him. This attachment exists only in the officer's imagination and, one by one, each is disillusioned by the coldness and even hatred of the troops.

The difference between the professional and the amateur officer's attitude toward his charges is also a traditional one in the American military establishment. General Pershing, for example, regarded the army as a machine to be operated efficiently; General Wood, the medical officer who became Chief of Staff, saw it as a collection of human beings, "gallant, lovable, wonderful . . . according to the leadership given them."[15] In the latest generation of American war novels this most potent of myths is laid to rest.

Jones and Heller destroy the belief that war is an exciting exercise. The stimulus of war derives from a terrible fear while the battle is actually in progress or in anticipation of battle and results in a correspondingly deep depression when the tension is relaxed. The surrealist scenes in *Catch-22* reflect the depression that succeeds the artificial stimulus of combat. Jones goes even further. After the first shock of battle the soldiers in *The Thin Red Line* find that war is essentially boring. Stripped of the myths of nobility, generosity, and comradeship, it becomes simply another big corporate operation in which the individual mechanically performs his part.

For many reasons one is led to believe that Vonnegut's *Mother Night* is the best of the American war novels of the absurd to appear in the late fifties and early sixties. Vonnegut avoids Heller's overextended attempts at humor, Jones's sometimes plodding symbolism, the admitted dilettantism of Harris's protagonist. The occasional flashes of humor and the generally ironic tone serve to underscore the poignancy of the contrast between Campbell's real desire for absolution and his ultimate fate. Campbell's flat overlooks four adjoining gardens (symbolic perhaps of the four races of the earth) in which children play hide-and-seek during the summer evenings. To call in their playmates at the end of a game they use the phrase "Olly, olly, oxenfree." Campbell dreams of a child calling such a phrase to him through the dusky evening to show that all is forgiven. Instead, one night there is a rap on his door at three o'clock, and he is dragged off by three (bogus) Israeli parachutists while a totally embittered old woman croons a phrase from the German death camps, "Leichanträger zu Wache," at him.

The international movement toward the absurd in war literature in the late fifties thus had a strong representation in the

United States. The powerful sense of individualism coupled with the tendency to tinker with a machine that was not working efficiently led the writers of the absurd to suggest that if the heroic mode of thought had twice culminated in a national disaster in less than fifty years, perhaps that mode of thought should be abandoned. Also, freedom from a militarist tradition allowed writers and intellectuals to junk an unworkable set of attitudes and begin anew with radically different concepts. The Europeans limited themselves to a statement of the absurdity of war; in the United States, simultaneously with the Kennedy regime's new departures in national strategic policy and the vitality of the pop art movement, the humane figure of the nonhero emerged. The bomb may have introduced an era of national funk, but in the end it also stimulated a peculiarly American reconciliation with the dangers of the nuclear age.

14. THE NONHERO

The emergence of the nonhero marks the complete reorientation of values in the American war novel in the period after World War II. In classical terms the hero is a Promethean figure embodying the enduring elements of the human spirit—a man that faces adversity without flinching and is ready to strike heaven in the face, to curse the gods and be destroyed. The nonhero, while remaining the center of the action, has a personality that is less inspiring. He tends not to fit into the pattern of the leader or the martyr and to devote himself to the principle of staying alive rather than sacrificing himself in a noble cause. Where Prewitt remains steadfast in the face of persecution and death, Yossarian contents himself with signing "Washington Irving" to the enlisted men's mail, and Jacob Epp writes "They should have let the South secede" on the mirrors in the latrine.

Prewitt was probably the last classic hero in the American war novel; he had the nobility of character and devotion to abstract ideals which delineate the type. Perhaps Robert Jordan in *For Whom the Bell Tolls* was another. In the novels written during and after World War II the heroic cast of thought begins to disappear. The jingoism of Jeffrey Wilson in John Marquand's *So Little Time* gives way to Nathaniel Hicks's realism in *Guard of Honor*: "Were there, perhaps, temporary wartime restrictions on getting what you worked for? No. Not if you could face the too-little-faced fact that war really brought you nothing that peace, mere living, couldn't eventually bring."[1] At about the same time that Cozzens was writing *Guard of Honor,* John F. Kennedy—fresh from the wars and not yet entered into politics—was saying in San Francisco, "We must face the fact that people have not been horrified by war to a sufficient extent. . . . War will exist until that distant day when the conscientious objector enjoys the same reputation and prestige that the warrior does today."[2] In other words, the attitude that culminated in the nonheroic outlook was already afoot in the forties; it was a process that emerged with increasing clarity throughout the decade of the fifties.

The type of the nonhero is already apparent in the character of Al Mannix in Styron's *The Long March:* "The man with the back unbreakable, the soul of pity, . . . great unshatterable vessel of longing, lost in the night, astray at midcentury in the never endingness of war,"[3] who has "suffered once, that 'once' being, in his own words, 'once too goddam many, Jack.' "[4] Malcolm Cowley said of those Americans who went to World War II: "Almost all of them agreed that Hitler and the Japanese had to be stopped, but they couldn't understand why somebody else than they, individually, shouldn't have done the stopping."[5] This attitude was perfected throughout the postwar period in characters like Mannix until it culminated in the nonheroism of Yossarian, Stein, and Jacob Epp.

Yossarian barely concedes that Hitler and the Japanese must be stopped, or rather he does not differentiate between their totalitarianism and that of the United States. The traditional patriotic viewpoint—"The loss of a war is an ultimate and irreversible fact; the impairment of a given civil liberty may be considered as the necessary sacrifice of a part for the sake of the whole, and even then a purely temporary affair as a matter of military expediency"[6]—is not acceptable to the nonhero, especially since he is painfully aware that the civil liberty which stands in danger of being impaired is his right to go on living. In any case, in his experience the question of who should stop the enemy becomes irrelevant. It is this disparity between the heroic or traditional and the nonheroic modes of thought that underlies the suggestion of madness in the novels of the absurd; it is fundamental to the neurotic logic of "Catch-22" and is also the basis for Jacob Epp's release from the army on a Section Eight. To the military establishment the nonhero must be insane, and vice versa. Thus in Deich's *The Sanity Inspectors* the psychiatrist-hero certifies the trainee pilots as being "insane" because they share his desire to live while the "sane" world is in the process of destroying itself.

Yet the actions and attitudes of the nonhero, although they conflict with accepted patterns of conduct, are not selfish or cowardly. Rather they represent a new approach to the problem of individuality in a world where traditional values, especially the concept of heroic action, have become deceptive. Norman Podhoretz's comment—"Heroism as Bellow envisages it in *Dangling Man* would consist in accepting the full burden of time and place, refusing to hold oneself aloof, and yet managing not to be overwhelmed or annihilated"[7]—is particularly applicable as well to the characters of Yossarian, Stein, and Epp. Their desire to participate fully in the events of their time is what distinguishes them clearly from the characters in the World War I novels of protest. In the works of Hemingway and Dos Passos the protagonists retreated into a silent despair; in the works of Heller and

Jones they turn outward to humanity. In this sense Mailer's *The Naked and the Dead* is atavistic; its solipsism suggests that it is in many ways the last of the World War I novels rather than the first important novel of World War II, as it is so often called. Mailer's characters resemble Henry or Hicks or Mattock in their isolation from their fellows, whereas in the characteristic novels of World War II there is a growing tendency to form a bond of comradeship which eventually culminates in the humanitarian attitudes of the nonheroes of the absurd.

On the other hand, it is the desire to live fully that causes the nonhero to break with the institutions of his society. As Vance Ramsey has pointed out, the nonhero may eventually become a victim, but he is never a pathetic victim;[8] the scene of cathartic destruction is not for him. This aspect of the nonheroic character is further illustrated by contrast with a remark made about *From Here to Eternity:* "Jones . . . suggests that men are responsible first for establishing and maintaining their personal or individual integrity, and second for establishing and maintaining the integrity of their relations in society and the physical world."[9] In Prewitt, the classic hero, these two considerations have almost equal importance; he jealously preserves his personal integrity, but he also strives to meet the requirements of army life, to "play by the rules." The nonhero, however, centers all his attention on the first consideration (personal integrity) and completely disregards the second, at least insofar as it concerns his relationship with the military establishment.

In contrast with the traditional American obsession with winning, to the nonheroes of the absurd, winning is utterly unimportant. To them the conflict is an internal one; living or dying depends on the individual's ability to evaluate the ruthlessness and absurdity of the system and stand in opposition to it or, better still, opt out of the system entirely. The nonhero accepts the idea that the hazards of war may be rooted in the nature of life itself, or at least in the organization of society, but he feels that during his lifetime he must not allow himself to be exposed to those hazards.

The outlook of these novelists is focused on human values. It has been said of Claes Oldenburg, an artist whose work became recognized while the novels of the absurd were being published, that his paintings are "impregnated with humanity." The same quality pervades the novels of the absurd. Jones does not refer to the enemy as "Nips" or "Japs" or even "Japanese" but insistently as "Japanese *men.*" Yossarian is supremely indifferent to the ideals of duty and honor but intensely interested in the welfare of Nately's whore's kid sister. Jacob Epp, baffled by the questions of war and peace, memorizes four simple sentences: *"Ich bin ihr Freund. . . . Schiessen Sie nicht. Das Ganze war ein Irrtum. Ich mochte es erklären*—I am your friend. Do not shoot. It was all a mistake. I can explain."[10]

This same concentration on the preeminence of life appears in Randall Jarrell's poem "The Sick Nought":

> Were you worth, soldiers, all that people said
> To be spent so willingly? Surely your one theory, to live,
> Is nonsense to the practice of the centuries.[11]

It is essentially this question that the novelists of the absurd seek to answer. In the face of the forces of tradition and social organization, Yossarian, Jacob Epp, and Captain Stein stage a revolt based on the simple premise that it is better to live than to die. The ideal concepts of right and wrong have become confusingly submerged in the process of international war and even more esoteric in the context of nuclear theorizing. Even someone as intelligent as Jacob Epp is baffled by the conflicting demands made on him by state and society: "He could not explain, as promised, the sentiment his heart's anguish had not yet translated to his tongue: as he would be neither oppressed nor oppressor, so now his heart renounced killing equally with dying."[12] For someone like Mess Sergeant Maynard Storm in *The Thin Red Line* the frustrations of modern war are even less capable of being put into words. He falls back on the fundamental, existential concept of doing what he can for the living: "There would be the evening meal to prepare for this stranger company here. His cooks stared at him as if he'd gone mad, but he didn't care. Fuck all that! Fuck everything! Feed men!"[13]

The realization that life is the fundamental condition for significant action underlies Captain Stein's unashamed acceptance of being relieved of his command and his frank gratification at being sent back to Washington. To the absurd logic of "Catch-22" Yossarian opposes his own argument that if everyone refused to fight there would be no more war. All of the novels, including Vonnegut's *Mother Night,* offer a variation on the theme of a "deal" offered to the nonhero by the establishment in exchange for silence. Stein and Campbell accept the deal, Epp has it forced upon him, and Yossarian refuses—only to carry out his own plan of escape. In each case the suggestion is that the reasons offered for accepting or refusing the deal are less important than the fact itself. Like the concept of the romance of warfare, the idea that one must justify his desire to live is swept into discard.

The apparently selfish and ignoble quality of nonheroic conduct has drawn the fire of some critics still attuned to traditional values. On the general subject of the human condition in the nuclear age Sidney Hook has said, "It seems to me that survival at all costs is not among the values of the West. . . . The free man is one who in certain situations refuses to accept life if it means spiritual degradation. The man who declares that survival at all costs is the end of existence is morally dead."[14] In the specific area of the war novel, Joseph Heller has been criticized for writing a novel whose hero wants only "to be left alone so that he may feed like the python and try to match the sexual prowess of the Japanese beetle."[15]

In fact, both of these comments distort the purpose of the novelists of the absurd because they disregard the objectives the nonhero is seeking. For one thing, as Leslie Fiedler has pointed out,[16] survival at all costs *has* become one of the values of the West. The nonhero does try to say that "survival at all costs is the end of existence" without being "morally dead." Most important of all, for characters like Yossarian and Jacob Epp the choice is not a simple case of "spiritual degradation" versus death; to them the spiritual degradation would result from continuing to serve the establishment when they know it is corrupt. Their purpose is to find a *tertium quid,* a life that involves neither heroic death nor involvement in the system.

The condemnation of the apparent selfishness of these men inevitably overlooks the fact that they are also genuine heroes in the traditional sense. Stein leads his company with bravery and devotion in the fierce battle for Guadalcanal. Campbell is motivated at least in part by a love of truth and justice and a romantic sense of daring. Epp enlists for the high purpose of serving his country, and Yossarian has flown "straight and level into the flak" on seventy missions. Insofar as these novels deal with the real events of World War II, the protagonists are highly endowed with the qualities of loyalty and heroism. As Norman Podhoretz has noted, "Heller is simply not prepared to say that World War II was a fraud, having nothing whatever to do with ideals or values."[17] On the contrary, the war forces the nonheroes to examine their ideals and values for the first time; but at the point where these novels begin to treat war as an enduring phenomenon, the protagonists adopt the only attitude that assures them of a continued existence. As Yossarian says to Major Danby, "I've been fighting all along to save my country. Now I'm going to fight a little to save myself";[18] when Danby protests, he says, "I'm not running *away* from my responsibilities. I'm running *to* them."[19]

The nonhero, moreover, tends to be a purely American phenomenon. The good soldier Schweik after all is not a nonhero but a *persona* like Swift's Gulliver; his idiotic delight in army life is the basis of Hasek's satire on militarism. While Helmut Kirst's Gunner Asch has an outlook similiar to Yossarian's, in the end he goes on fighting; and the medical officer in *The Sanity Inspectors* is finally destroyed by the S.S. When Pierre Boulle's *The Bridge on the River Kwai* appeared on the screen, the nonheroic figure of Shears was an innovation for the American film. The book itself had no such figure.

Similarly the belief in the possibility of a *tertium quid,* a mode of existence that is neither heroic nor cowardly, is a specifically American contribution to the war novel of the absurd. One critic has said that Yossarian heads for Sweden as the promised land, but he is almost sure to be disappointed. Not all the women will surrender; liquor may be expensive; he may have to work; "Yet, Sweden remains valid as an idea, . . . man in his desperation may still desire Paradise."[20] Perhaps all the novelists of the absurd—European as well as American—still desire Paradise, but only the Americans suggest that it is attainable. In other words, "the territories" still exist for the American nonhero, as they did for Huckleberry Finn. Stein escapes to the fleshpots of Washington; Jacob Epp is saved in order that he may have a tranquil career as a high-school history teacher; even though Campbell chooses to kill himself while he is in the Israeli prison, he is given a clear-cut chance to survive and go scot-free. His Blue Fairy Godmother does identify himself in time to save Campbell if he had so desired. In the United States, even when warfare and the military establishment have come to be treated as absurdities, something of the national optimism is still reflected in the personality of the nonhero.

15. BLACK HUMOR

The mood of hopelessness arising from the prospect of nuclear war in the fifties was heightened by the knowledge that, in keeping with recent practice, such an attack would undoubtedly be directed at the civilian population as well as at military installations. Little faith could be placed in the ability of the government to restrict a nuclear war entirely to military targets. Just as the theoreticians' concept of a purely controlled response would probably become an all-out attack when one side saw itself losing, so the idea of a purely "counterforce" war seemed to exist only in the realm of pure theory. The Strategic Air Command's doctrine of the "optimum mix"—a policy of including cities as well as military installations in targeting a country in order to instill maximum terror in the enemy—became public knowledge[1] and hardly tended to reassure the civilian population as to the probable result of a nuclear attack.

The attempts on the part of government agencies to approach this problem and analyze it rationally tended only to isolate the analyst from reality and, if anything, intensify the horror of the subject. Some of the most chilling literature written in the twentieth century are the factual studies made of nuclear strategy and probable effects of a nuclear attack on civilian populations. For example, one analyst estimates that a successful enemy attack on fifty metropolitan centers would result in critical damage to at least 40 percent of the population, 50 percent of the key facilities, and 60 percent of the industry. But this would still leave 90–100 million survivors.[2] Ironically most of this literature is intended to reassure the reader,[3] but an essay like Herman Kahn's "Some Comments on Controlled War"[4] or Kenneth Thompson's "Nuclear Weapons" produces an overpowering sensation that the writer has forgotten he is dealing with human lives and that symbols and statistics have obliterated the real significance of what he is saying.

The effect of the cold war anxieties on the arts was described by William Faulkner in his 1950 Nobel Prize speech: "Our tragedy today is a general and universal physical fear so long sustained by now that we can even bear it." He went on to say that this craven physical fear had sapped the initiative of the writers so that they no longer dealt with the classic and enduring themes of "love and honor and pity and pride and compassion and sacrifice."[5] Not surprisingly the terror and apathy described by Faulkner modulated into a comic mood. It has been noted that the "notoriously short life of the great periods of tragic drama" have resulted from the "powerful . . . human urge toward resolution" which results in a tendency for the tensions of tragedy to "modulate into a religious or quasi-religious or comic mood."[6] Certainly one of the dominant characteristics of the novels of the cold war has been the element of black humor.

Black humor, which takes for its subject the most tragic experiences of human existence, was effectively employed as part of the Allied propaganda campaign in World War II. Where World War I propaganda has been based to a large extent on overblown and poorly documented atrocity stories, Daniel Lerner says that Allied psychological warfare was based on the use of accurate factual information that would tend to produce despair in the enemy: "The propaganda of despair . . . was in fact the inclusive category of Sykewar output in World War II."[7] This element was also fundamental to Sykewar "humor," and its effect appeared in the *Galgenhumor* (gallows humor) of the German soldier himself. "The hallmark of the best German novels on the war is a bitter humor that in itself suggests the irrational nature of military life."[8] It is not surprising, therefore, to find this type of humor playing a major role in the American war novel at a time when the Americans themselves were faced with the "propaganda of despair."

Furthermore, the American situation (and perhaps that of the whole world) is complicated by the fact that the mechanism of government has grown so remote and complex that the individual feels an acute sense of disparity; i.e., he feels incapable of meaningfully affecting the course of events. It has been pointed out that in the field of foreign policy this results in mutually supporting feelings of awe and distrust. The average man feels that the government cannot explain the situation to him intelligibly and that it would not do so if it could.[9] These two factors—the awareness of frightful danger and the sense of impotence arising from the complexity and remoteness of the government—certainly underlie and contribute to the emergence of black humor as a prime component in the American war novel.

In the novels of the absurd the element of black humor reflects an attitude toward warfare roughly parallel to that expressed by Cummings in World War I. Essentially it is a means of coping with the horror of war, but it operates only in a negative sense;

it momentarily relieves the trauma but does not offer a consistent alternative to the social creed that requires the individual to participate in the slaughter.

Black humor is also a device employed to overcome two of the self-defeating effects of what Leslie Fiedler calls the "antiwar" novel—the novel of protest. Kenneth Burke has suggested that the novel of protest is not really effective as an instrument of antiwar sentiment; it may even serve as a basis for appeals to heroic sacrifice: "The greater the horror, the greater the thrill and honor of enlistment."[10] Burke adds that because of this effect, "the sly cartoonists of the *New Yorker* might possibly do most to discourage militarism."

If black humor helps deflate the appeal of danger, it also serves to overcome the numbness which results from repeated exposure to scenes of horror. The novelists of World War I had exhausted the capacity of their audience to respond to descriptions of mass slaughter. The novelists of the absurd selected black humor as "a technique that serves to lower the reader's defenses so that the full force of the horror may be felt"[11] in order to communicate with an audience that had become indifferent to the horrors of war.

Black humor, however, represents only one part of the outlook of the novelists of the absurd. Like Cummings they use it to provide an immediate respite from the experience or threat of war, but unlike Cummings and the other novelists of the First World War they do not lapse into despair and withdrawal; they also provide a unified and rather hopeful reaction to the situation. Thus when Jacob Epp, seeking sympathy, says to his battery commander, " 'My friend is dead. . . . Dead in a burning airplane between Salerno and Naples, Italy,' " Captain Dodd replies cynically, " 'That's what happens . . . when you fly around in burning airplanes.' "[12] Dodd is not merely seeking the soldier's traditional relief from horror; he is also trying to bring Epp to the point where he will recognize the futility of military service and the importance of living rather than dying. When Epp remonstrates with him, " 'How can you be so cruel when a man is dead?' " Dodd replies, " 'I'll tell you something even crueller . . . so you'll know the cruellest thing I know. I'll tell you a cruel thing if you want to know. You want to know things, don't you? You want to know the cruellest thing? You want to know what? . . . You next.' "[13]

In *The Thin Red Line* James Jones similarly uses black humor both to relieve the horror and baseness of war and to establish a point of departure from which he can move toward an alternative. The soldiers' mocking fashion show staged with the bloody shirt they find in the jungle, Big Queen's insane tug-of-war with the leg of the dead Japanese soldier in the lime-filled trench, and—most important of all—John Bell's jumbled, surrealistic amalgamation of the events of the war with his erotic imaginings about his wife (which do satirically culminate in his receiving a "Dear John" letter) are all in the black humor tradition.

Black humor is one of the main elements that link *The Thin Red Line* to Joseph Heller's *Catch-22*. It is possible for Heller to employ the element of black humor far more heavily than do either Jones or Mark Harris, simply because his story line is less realistic than theirs; from the outset it is subordinated to his wild flights of insane laughter. In fact this element characterizes *Catch-22;* every piece of seemingly innocuous wit culminates eventually in a glimpse of the dark horror that Heller and Yossarian strive to conceal. Periodically throughout the book the real world of the laughing American boys slides abruptly into the surrealism of Yossarian's depressing vision of the true nature of modern war. These transition points occur too frequently to be disregarded, and usually they take the form of an extension of a standard humorous situation. Thus Major Major Major's appointment as squadron commander, normally the occasion for good-natured pleasantries, turns the squadron into a howling bloodthristy mob; Milo Minderbinder's shopping jaunt around the Mediterranean, very much in the tradition of Mark Twain and O. Henry, becomes a purgatory of sleeplessness and alienation for Yossarian and Orr who are outside the system; the horror of Nately's death is linked with the weird interrogation of Chaplain Tappman; and the squadron's many hilarious furloughs in Rome culminate in Yossarian's nightmare walk through the streets of the city while every form of human brutality is perpetrated around him.

Jones and Harris use black humor sparingly, more or less as a counterpoint to the vivid realism of their story; but in Heller's novel, as in Vonnegut's *Mother Night,* it becomes a dominant element and almost an end in itself. It reached its climax in the bitter irony of the thought that flashes through Yossarian's mind as he stares at Snowden's dreadful wound: "Here was God's plenty, all right . . . liver, lungs, kidneys, ribs, stomach and bits of the stewed tomatoes Snowden had eaten that day for lunch. Yossarian hated stewed tomatoes."[14] The reader is led remorselessly, through Heller's manipulation of the various humorous techniques, to the ultimate realization that there is nothing laudable or good-natured about warfare.

Writing of the need for historians to reappraise strategy and military policy in the nuclear age, C. Vann Woodward has said, "The historic service that Cervantes performed with mockery in

1605, when he published the first volume of Don Quixote, three centuries after the advent of firearms, cannot with safety be deferred that long after the advent of nuclear weapons."[15] Perhaps it is not unreasonable to suggest that Joseph Heller is the Cervantes of the atomic era and Yossarian and Orr its Don Quixote and Sancho Panza.

16. THE WAR NOVEL AS POP ART

In *Catch-22* the realization that war is absurd manifested itself in the soldier's traditional black humor.

But the novelists of the absurd, especially James Jones, also gave voice to a mood that was peculiar to America in the sixties. The European novelists resorted to the bitterest of satire; the American novelists of the absurd tended to write in a style that was hip, deadpan, and sophisticated. In so doing they produced a literature that had a curious analogy to the visual arts in the same period and even to the new mood that was abroad in the realm of politics.

The late fifties produced the phenomenon of pop art in the United States, an art form restricted in the first instance to the work of five New York artists: Andy Warhol, Roy Lichtenstein, Tom Wesselman, James Rosenquist, and Claes Oldenburg. It is a form characterized primarily by the use of banal subject matter, orgiastic color, and gigantic scale. Like the existentialism of the novelists of the absurd and the political virility of the Kennedy regime, it represented a turning away from the indecisiveness and anxiety of the preceding decade and a reaction against the introversion of the abstract expressionists.

The abstract-expressionist painters created unique worlds within the limits of a canvas plane—worlds complete unto themselves without reference to any external reality. . . . Pop art, utilizing the same artistic freedoms, represents the opposite pole of expression. Abstract expressionism was a turning within, Pop art is a turning out.[1]

Having lived long enough in the shadow of a demoralizing fear, the artists and intellectuals of the New World decided to coexist with the threat by controlling those aspects of their lives that were capable of being controlled and by emphasizing the positive aspects of human existence. Of the pop art movement one writer has said, "Its standards were . . . determined . . . by a widespread decision to approach the contemporary world with a positive rather than negative attitude. . . . Pop Art's alternative to the emotional and technical impastoes of its immediate predecessor was clearly based on a tough, no-nonsense, no-preciosity, norefinement standard appropriate to the 1960s."[2] Going even farther back one can trace the emotional origins of the pop art movement in the shocked numbness of the generation that had experienced World War I. America's first exposure to full-scale war had overworked its capacity to give meaningful expression to the experience, and after World War II "the tear glands of the world dried up from over-use. It is this world for which Warhol is spokesman."[3] In the shadow of the nuclear peril an element of emotional shock commensurate with that induced by the First World War was threatening, and the artists chose to concentrate on an affirmation of life rather than on expressions of fear and despair.

It has long been accepted that there was an important link between the Dadaists and the expatriate American writers in the twenties; Dadaism reflected the mood of the "lost generation." In this sense it seems reasonable to argue that the pop art movement was generated by the conditions of the nuclear age and that specifically it was a product of the bomb. If the word "decisive" can be applied to the visual arts, then pop art is decisive. The strong black outlines and bright primary colors suggest a firmness and clarity of vision which supersedes the uncertainty and isolation of the work of the postwar artists. Roy Lichtenstein's blown-up comic strips are the prime example of pop art's clarity, simpleness, and strength; but the same aspects are found in the work of Andy Warhol, Tom Wesselman, and the others. In other words, it is possible to see in pop art a manifestation of the same spirit that characterizes the whole generation that grew up under the threat of the bomb.

Like the theme it expresses, the materials of pop art are commonplace—simple to the point of banality. They consist of familiar objects which until now have never been considered as having any artistic significance: automobiles, Brillo boxes, comic strips, hot dogs, motorcycle helmets. All these elements in the pop artist's stock share three essential characteristics: they are manufactured articles, they have been designed by anonymous artists, and they are directly related to some fundamental aspect of human life—eating, working, procreation, or entertainment. From this consideration several conclusions can be drawn. First, the pop artist has found a way to reconcile himself with the harsh facts of life in an industrial society. Pop art relies on a recognition of beauty in manufactured articles. Secondly, the anonymity of the components' original designers focuses attention on theme rather than personality. Finally, pop art focuses on the business of everyday living; it is intensely interested in human life at the most basic levels. At the same time it makes a sardonic comment on the values of modern American life.

In form, color, and organization pop art is vigorous, erotic, and surreal. Generally the technique of the pop artist depends on two principal factors: the collage or assemblage of familiar objects into new and striking forms and the expansion of a commonplace article to the point of surrealism. The *assemblage* aspect is important in that it depends on the artist's ability to present an idea while disregarding the origin of his materials. It marks the point at which the American artist turns toward the expression of an idea. The second technique, which is represented by the expansion of a comic strip panel to enormous size, focuses atttention on the link between popular taste and artistic vision. Usually in these paintings the details of the original comic strip or poster are simplified, colors are made clearer and outlines sharpened. This, combined with the vast scale, produces a weird dreamlike impression similar to that of a painting by Salvador Dali. The comic strip or poster becomes a link with the world of dreams and imagination, with a curiously erotic effect.

At the same time that the pop artist was responding to the fear and fecklessness of the fifties in an idiom that was based on firmness, clarity, and devotion to the principle of life (even when it remained uncommitted or ironic as to the values of the consumer society), and when a new sense of confidence was emanating from Washington, the novelists of the absurd also began to employ pop art techniques to convey their message. In *Something about a Soldier, Mother Night,* and *Catch-22* the link with pop art is provided by the strong element of surrealism. Jacob Epp, returning to his barracks at night, finds his ideal of an American soldier, Sergeant Toat, grinning like a death's-head in the moonlight and calling him "Jewboy." In *Mother Night* the woman whom Campbell had loved and who was killed during the war reappears in a ghostly fashion, exists briefly as a dream or a figment of his imagination, and is destroyed in a nightmare sequence. In *Catch-22* the dream element pervades the entire book. In conjunction with the time lapses, exaggerations, improbabilities, and confused sequence of events it contributes to a sense of unreality arising out of commonplace circumstances.

The surrealist aspect manifests itself in *The Thin Red Line* in John Bell's irrational song "Don't monkey around with death" which is essentially gibberish that Bell recites in order to forget the terror and monotony of war—and in the reaction of C-for-Charlie Company to the dead man who suddenly appears in their lines: "There was muttering. C-for-Charlie did not feel they had done anything to deserve him, and they resented his being palmed off on them. Several men who cautiously approached to within six or seven yards of him returned to say that he smelled."[4] Like the soldier in white or the dead man in Yossarian's tent, his origin and identity are apparently unknown; he is at once commonplace and supernatural.

The prime example of pop art technique in the American war novel is *The Thin Red Line.* In *The Bridge on the River Kwai* Pierre Boulle had used a monotonous repetition of the phrase "Number One" to give the effect of men playing at war without realizing its horrors; James Jones employs this and other pop art techniques in his novel. First of all, *The Thin Red Line* is a clear example of assemblage; it is a pastiche composed of elements taken from many other war stories. A brief catalog of some of the elements that have appeared in previous war novels includes the resemblances between the souvenir-hunting expedition and Norman Mailer's description of American soldiers robbing the dead in *The Naked and the Dead;* the campaign map and Mailer's map of Anopopei in *The Naked and the Dead;* Charlie Dale's collection of gold teeth and that of Sergeant Martinez in *The Naked and the Dead;* the march to the bivouac and Corporal Fife's insubordination en route and similar events in William Styron's *The Long March;* Colonel Tall and General Emerson in *The Young Lions;* the theft of the tommy guns and a similar theft in Leon Uris's *Battle Cry;* the regular Japanese bombing run also described as "Washing Machine Charlie" in *Battle Cry;* Bell's song and "the reenlistment blues" in Jones's earlier *From Here to Eternity;* and —most obvious of all—the metamorphosis of the characters in *From Here to Eternity.* In *The Thin Red Line* Master Sergeant Warden becomes Master Sergeant Welsh, Mess Sergeant Maylon Stark becomes Mess Sergeant Maynard Storm, and Robert E. Lee Prewitt becomes simply Witt. Also, where the pop artists selected manufactured objects whose impersonality reflected the impersonality of modern life, Jones composes his dialogue around the most impersonal of conversational elements—army slang and profanity. He emphasizes the banal nature of this material by the platitudinous repetition of phrases like "C-for-Charlie," "imperial quart," and "longnosed, mean, and meanlooking Italian exec."

Finally, the pop art element appears in the emphasis on war as corporate action or big business in both *Catch-22* and *The Thin Red Line.* Death is immanent and real for Yossarian and the men in C-for-Charlie Company, but the process that culminated in their being in the presence of death seems to them mechanical and inhuman. The preeminence of commerce is emphasized to a degree unprecedented in the war novel. The combat scenes in *Catch-22* are balanced by the managerial and commercial rivalry of Milo Minderbinder and ex-Pfc Wintergreen; in *The Thin Red Line* there is Sergeant Welsh's insistence that the war is being fought for "property, property, all for property." In this sense the authors of these works have transposed the war novel into the idiom of the sixties; war is no longer seen as the result of human passion or idealism but as a product of the same industrialized society that provides the pop artist with his crash helmets, Brillo boxes, and soup cans.

What then is the message of the pop art movement, and how is this message reflected in the novels of the absurd? The message of pop art seems to be that life, even in an industrialized society, is good when one considers that the alternative is death. The follies of the corporate state and the consumer society may be appalling, but the commentary on those follies need not be bitter. The deadpan presentation can also be effective, and it leaves open the possibility of progress in new directions.

Since the time of Walt Whitman and Carl Sandburg the American artist has been enthralled by the concepts of size and energy, of power and production. The pop art movement in a way represents a return to peculiarly American interests. The livid colors; the perception of beauty even in the banal; the emphasis on food, sex, and speed are all elements that focus the attention on living. In a society that had existed for more than a decade in the paralytic fear of death, this is an important emphasis, and it is fundamental to the novels of the absurd.

The vitality of the pop art element in novels like *Catch-22* and *The Thin Red Line* is in keeping with the essentially optimistic nature of the nonhero. At the moment when the destructive power of "Catch-22" seems to have become omnipresent through the merger of ex-Pfc Wintergreen and M and M Enterprises, the news of Orr's escape to Sweden regenerates faith in the power of human beings to survive and to perform meaningful actions.[5] If Orr can paddle all the way to Sweden in a rubber dinghy, then Clevinger is probably still hiding in his cloud waiting for the war to end, and perhaps there is hope for everyone.

The pop art aspect provides a mode of expression for the optimism in the American character; it also is the means by which American war novelists could move toward technical improvement. The first spate of war novels after 1945 had been largely factual accounts of combat experience. Although they were accurate in detail and immediately satisfying to a public hungry for war stories, ultimately they failed to transmit the true atmosphere of the war. The novels of the absurd made up this deficiency by emphasizing what could be called the "reality of the surreal."

The works of the absurd are firmly anchored in real life (the island of Pianosa can be seen on any map of Italy, and Mailer has said of *The Thin Red Line* that it would serve admirably as a textbook of infantry tactics).[6] They also add a new dimension to the treatment of war in literature. It has been said that "what every ex-military man misses in so many novels to come out of World War II and the Korean War is the sense of grotesqueness of the situation, the irrationality and inadequacy of the means for survival, and in general a feeling of mingled terror and unreality."[7] The weird passages in *The Thin Red Line* and *Catch-22* are a response to this deficiency; the surrealistic horror of a scene like that in which the familiar path to the bathing beach assumes a nightmare atmosphere[8] helps the reader understand the depression which follows the artificial stimulus of danger.

The same surrealistic technique is employed to correct the notion that army regulations are a large but harmless source of humor. "Catch-22," for example, which stipulates that if a man is afraid to die he is sane and must therefore fly more missions, is not really very different from that aspect of the induction procedure which requires the draftee to go through the formality of volunteering for service. At United States Army recruiting centers the officer in charge tells the draftees, " 'Those *wishing* to enlist in the U.S. Army will so signify by taking one step forward. . . .' Draftees are forced to answer the call or risk imprisonment."[9] Here again the absurd is the only adequate medium for reproducing certain real aspects of military life.

The novels of the absurd thus are the American contribution to a worldwide movement in war literature that began to appear in the late fifties. Within the general framework that treats warfare as an absurdity, at least two distinctly American contributions were made. One was the figure of the nonhero, apparently selfish and unpatriotic but in reality optimistic and humane; the other was the adaptation to the war novel of the vigor and toughness of the pop art movement. While the absurd represented a new approach to the subject of war, it also provided the means by which traditional war literature could be perfected. There is no reason to believe that the absurd will necessarily remain the dominant mode of dealing with warfare in fiction, but when it appeared in the early sixties it did provide a useful corrective to a certain hawkish sentiment that was becoming increasingly evident in the United States. More important, the novels of the absurd suggest that the traditional American optimism has not been overwhelmed by the fears and anxieties of the cold war.

CONCLUSION:
THE INDESTRUCTIBLE THEME

In one of his essays George Santayana implies a symbolic relationship between the Robinson Crusoe myth and American society,[1] a metaphor that is particularly appropriate in relation to the history of American military and foreign policy. The pioneer, cast ashore with the wreckage of old beliefs and policies, tried to live peacefully in the wilderness; at the same time the exigencies and the freedom of the frontier inculcated in him a spirit of innovation and independence that would characterize his reaction to new circumstances when they arose. In this context Hiroshima was the footprint in the sand. From that point onward the American had to live permanently with the threat of personal danger and help solve the problems that face the entire world. The factors that permitted a unique American approach to the problems of foreign policy were paralleled by internal conditions which governed the nation's attitude toward the military establishment. It has been said that the dislike of militarism and the military establishment in America "has a saga-like quality. . . . Our wars have been so spaced and have been so waged that every generation of citizens has experienced or has touched hands with those who suffered the collision of tyro and professional soldier. Out of the sum of individual adventures or the telling of them has been compounded the prejudice of common men."[2] In a nation where tradition and aristocratic privilege count for nothing, it was to be expected that the familiar theme of men in arms would be treated in a new light.

Since 1880 the theme of warfare has attracted the attention of practically every major novelist in the United States; the writing of a war novel has become a form of apprenticeship uniting authors whose prime interests lay in other areas. As Leslie Fiedler has noted, since the 1920s at least the war novel has become "a standard way of starting a literary career."[3] In some cases the war novel has been the springboard from which a successful literary career was launched. The first achievements of Stephen Crane, John Dos Passos, and William Faulkner lay in this field, as did those of James Jones, Herman Wouk, Irwin Shaw, and Norman Mailer. In other cases—like the work of Herman Melville, Willa Cather, Ernest Hemingway, John Marquand, and James Gould Cozzens—the war novel was a significant addition to an already established reputation.

Perhaps the most bizarre, if least successful, example of the American propensity to write war novels was the case of Frederick Schiller Faust—better known as Max Brand although he had seventeen other *noms de plume*. It is estimated that Faust wrote approximately 500 novels between 1917 and 1939; in one peak period he wrote a novel every ten days for a decade. Almost all these novels were sold to pulp magazines at the prime rate of five cents a word. Although he lived like a prince in a Florentine villa, Faust also thought of himself as a scholar and a poet; he read Homer and Dante in the original Greek and Italian and was perfectly conversant with all aspects of English literature. When editors refused to give serious consideration to this aspect of his work and character, Faust decided to write a magnum opus—" 'one really meaningful book' about a company of American soldiers from their training to their behavior under fire." He managed to have himself accredited as a war correspondent with the American troops in Italy in order to gather material for his novel; in May 1944 he was killed while participating in a night attack on a German position.[4]

In any case actual wartime service was not a necessary qualification for authorship; the theme was familiar and important enough to merit the attention of combatant and noncombatant alike. Crane established the precedent of noncombatant authorship in America with *The Red Badge of Courage,* and from that time on the theme of warfare has been fair game for all. If only one American writer, James Jones, can be regarded solely as a war novelist in the sense that all his major works *(From Here to Eternity, Some Came Running, The Pistol,* and *The Thin Red Line)* touch on the subject to a greater or lesser degree, it should also be noted that Jones is one of the most enduring authors to appear in the United States in the last thirty years. At its peak the theme was good for more than a single effort on the part of a given author; at least one respectable literary career was based upon it.

What are the reasons for American preoccupation with war literature? This obsession seems to have derived partly from the manner in which the American continent itself came to give expression to some aspects of the human character. Many writers have insisted on the primacy of the hunting instinct in man, as opposed to the tendency to become domesticated and agricultural.[5] Lewis Mumford has developed the argument that America provided an outlet for man's desire to return to nature and that once freed of the bonds of European civilization the settler quickly succumbed to the irrepressible hunting instinct.[6]

Certainly America is one of the few technologically advanced countries in the world where hunting is widely practiced. It seems reasonable to argue that since war is only a specialized form of the hunt, the two should hold a special interest for the citizens of the United States. One critic has said, "The novels of World War II, like the literature of any war, have for the most part been attempts to understand and give artistic form to experiences which magnify the violence and chaos of human existence."[7] In a country where for 300 years the relaxation of traditional restraints combined with the positive need to wrest a living from the wilderness, the elements of chaos and violence have come to be especially pertinent. One sees the duality of hunting and warfare presented with special clarity in a work like Hemingway's *In Our Time,* where scenes of war counterpoint scenes from the wilderness, or in Mailer's *Why Are We In Viet Nam?* where the question posed by the title is explored in the atmosphere of an Alaskan big game hunt.

Another aspect of warfare that corresponds to the frontier instinct is the element of simplicity vis-à-vis problems of morality. Saul Bellow's waspish comment that Americans "are unpractised in introspection, and therefore badly equipped to deal with opponents whom they cannot shoot like big game or outdo in daring,"[8] like James Balwin's claim that "American he-men [are totally unprepared] for anything that [can] not be settled with a club or a fist or a gun,"[9] focuses attention on the American tendency to seek the simple solution. This tendency is also reflected in the standard denouement of the Western movie; war can be seen as a variation on the scene at the OK Corral, where the sheriff solves the most complicated issues of the community with a blazing sixshooter. In both cases the most bewildering paradox can be reduced to a simple test of strength and courage. As Reinhold Niebuhr says, the Americans understand economic interest and the threat of pure military force but are completely "mystified by the endless complexities of human motives and the varied compounds of ethnic loyalties, cultural traditions, social hopes, envies and fears which enter into the policies of nations."[10]

War literature also is reminiscent of the masculinity of pioneering life. Edmund L. Volpe has noted that "James Jones's fictional terrain is limited to that peculiar all-male world governed by strictly masculine interests, attitudes, and values."[11] This observation is in keeping with Fiedler's comments in *Love and Death in the American Novel* on the curiously strong element of celibacy in American letters. Volpe adds that in Jones's novels the army is treated as the last frontier of rugged masculine individual-ism: "Prewitt wants to be a thirty-year man because the raw violence, the drunken sprees, the sex without responsibility, the demands on physical endurance and technical skill express and challenge his maleness."[12]

All these factors combined have produced an almost poignant treatment of the soldier by the American novelist. Mailer, for example, harks back constantly to his army days when life was both dangerous and morally simplified. His later novels typically revolve around the adventures of a soldier or ex-soldier wandering numbly through the horrors of civilian life. When he deals in reportage, as in *Miami and the Siege of Chicago* (1968), he is pre-occupied with organizing defensive perimeters and rallying his troops; like a latter-day Hemingway he dreams of himself as the tough officer and, also like Hemingway, he obsessively raises the question of how he will react in moments of danger.

One can trace the thread of masculinity, danger, and courage from Mailer back through Hemingway to Crane. In *The Red Badge of Courage* and "The Veteran" Crane shook off his charac-teristic pessimism to create a hero whom he endowed with every-thing a man could ask in life: youthful adventure, comrade-ship, and heroic action; then a happy domestic scene, long life, and finally a quick and heroic death. In Crane, Hemingway, Mailer, and many other American authors one finds works that reflect a bitter appreciation of American life; but in each of these authors one also finds an almost envious evocation of a dream of bravery, simplicity, and devotion. Taken together these attitudes represent the basic paradox of American war literature: the au-thors tend to admire the idea of the soldierly virtues while they detest the fact of the military establishment. Even where the antipathy toward the armed forces is muted, one still perceives the esteem in which the authoritarian figure of the officer is held. Thus Wouk suddenly turns *The Caine Mutiny* into an accolade for men like Commander Queeg, Marquand underlines the man-ner in which Melville Goodwin resembles Horatius at the bridge, and Cozzens suggests that the general officer is a race apart.

The war novel has thus provided a medium of expression for some important themes that are especially related to the American character; but these novels also reflect a peculiarly American atti-tude toward the idea of warfare itself. America is a new society, lacking any real military tradition, and there is no reason for it to conform to the outlook of the older western societies. For the first century of its existence the Republic produced no enduring war literature whatever. The landmark authors of this period—Nathaniel Hawthorne, Edgar Allan Poe, Walt Whitman, Mark

Twain, and even Henry James—concerned themselves with the dark questions of guilt or innocence and of violence between individuals in society, themes which seem to have a special import to the American mind.

Furthermore, writers like Tom Paine and Henry Thoreau became part of the national mythos long before a war novel was written by giving expression to the nonconformist aspect of the American character. When Ralph Waldo Emerson said that each man "must sit solidly at home, and not suffer himself to be bullied by kings or empires,"[13] he was using the term "kings or empires" as a metaphor for history; but the spirit of the passage is reflected in the attitudes of later fictional heroes. All the most memorable characters in the American war novels—Henry Fleming, Lieutenant Henry, Robert E. Lee Prewitt, Yossarian—are obsessed with the idea of their individuality. If American society in general offers a special threat to this aspect of existence, then the war novel—or more specifically the antiwar novel—is the perfect medium for working out a response to the threat, since it pits the individual against the organization that above all others specializes in reducing men to interchangeable parts of a machine.

The pacifist and nonheroic outlook of characters like Yossarian and Captain Stein also reflects a long-standing American tradition. They are like the Revolutionary soldiers of whom it was said, "Their greatest Study is to Rub through their Tower [tour] of Duty with whole Bones."[14] This attitude also underlay the enthusiastic response to the keynote speech at the 1916 Democratic convention when Governor Glynn of New York told a cheering audience that "one could be patriotic and pacifistic, that it was the historic American policy to submit to great provocation and historically un-American to go to war over it."[15] In the sixties one saw a reincarnation of this attitude in organizations like the Yippies and the Students for a Democratic Society.

Another factor which complicates the writing of war literature is the shift that has taken place in the American attitude toward warfare and the military establishment since 1945. The postwar period saw the merging of the categories of civilian and military: " 'professional' was the one term seized upon by newsmen and observers to describe the peculiar psychology of the Korean fighting man as distinguished from his World War II counterpart."[16] At the same time that the civilian in uniform was becoming less distinguishable from his professional counterpart, the events of the nuclear age were forcing the latter to adopt the practices and outlook of the big civilian corporation; conversely, the civilian businessman adopted the methods, the vocabulary, and the outlook of the professional soldier. Vance Packard has observed: "The orderliness of the corporate world has its counterpart in—and presumably was inspired by—the officers' way of life in the military organization. . . . It is hardly a coincidence that corporate officials take special pleasure in being known as 'Captains of Industry.' "[17] The professional officer still exists, but he tends to be a "military manager" dealing with technical and human problems not much different from those encountered by teachers, diplomats, and businessmen. The profession of arms with its special problems of bravery, judgment, and sacrifice has now either disappeared or is practiced on a level too limited to generate great war literature.

The writing of war novels based on experiences of past wars will probably continue, despite this disappearance of the professional soldier as a unique and major influence in national life and also despite the second principal effect of the bomb: in the nuclear age the dire threat of destruction has created a new attitude toward warfare. Morris Janowitz noted that both the self-image and the public image of the soldier have worsened since the advent of thermonuclear warfare which made the concept of glory gained in combat ridiculous. Even the skirmishes and tensions of the cold war have not been sufficient to make military service glamorous to Americans; they do not want any part of it.[18] Recent indications suggest that Janowitz's assessment of the situation has remained accurate. For example, in the March 1968 edition of *Atlantic* it was observed that John Wayne had difficulty in finding a studio that would contract to distribute his film *The Green Berets:* "The word in Hollywood was that the subject—the war in Viet Nam—was 'too controversial.' "[19] That same month an article in *Punch* stated: "Some while back *Newsweek* reported that not all American comic artists were keen to feature Viet Nam. It was too much of an infantryman's war; they preferred to exercise their skills on big-scale, free-ranging hardware. Besides, the theme of big guy versus little guy created 'problems of reader empathy.' "[20]

It has been seen that the attitudes toward warfare and the military establishment expressed in American war novels do tend to vary from those found in the war novels of other countries. Perhaps the most important single divergence lies in the fact that the enlisted man, not the officer, is almost invariably the protagonist in the American novel. There is also the basic sense of alienation toward war as an institution, especially in those novels written before 1952. Fundamental to almost all of these works is the idea that war is not an integral part of life. In the novels written from about 1952 onward there is a growing realization that war is a permanent phenomenon; in the earlier works it is possible to make a strong contrast with the European war novel in which war is accepted as a recurring phenomenon. The fictional European soldier complains about the discomforts and stupidities of war but not about its endemic quality or the hierarchical structure of the military organization itself; to him war is part of life, and the military organization has strong analogies with the social structure he knew as a civilian. For the American, however, war is an aberration that he hopes may be permanently ended, and the authoritarian military organization is a standing insult to the most dearly cherished concepts of liberty and individuality.

On the other hand, it must also be said that there are points of resemblance between the war novels written in the United States and those written in other countries. The horror expressed in Thomas Boyd's *Through the Wheat* at the colossal follies of the western front had its counterpart in scores of novels written at about the same time on the other side of the Atlantic. The convergence in tone and mood of the American and European war novels becomes most marked in the fifties and after; it is during this decade that the enormities of the cold war begin to override what once were distinguishing characteristics. In *Mother Night* the deaths of Helga and Resi juxtaposed to the continued existence of Mrs. Epstein suggest that human love must die in our world while bitterness and hate—i.e., Mother Night—lives on. But the war novel of the absurd is an international phenomenon. Whatever contrast there may be at this point between the European and the American war novel derives from the fact that for the Americans an element of hope, however slim, still exists; there is still the belief that the nonhero can survive.

Finally there is the question of which direction the American war novel is likely to take in the future. It has been argued that the novel, as genre, is not suited to the treatment of the theme of war. Bernard Bergonzi has said, "The novel . . . is not an easy form in which to accommodate heroic figures; its natural bias is so much to the realistic, the typical, the ordinary, that the presence of any figure of conspicuous stature and virtue is liable to set up ironic tensions";[21] it will serve as a medium for reminiscence or memoir but not for idealization. The tendency in British war literature since the Second World War has been to support this claim, as the heroic possibilities of the war novel seemed to become rapidly exhausted. Yet the supposition may not be universally valid. In America there exists a special interest in "the realistic, the typical, the ordinary" which may allow American novelists to deal successfully with the theme of war without necessarily evoking the heroic image. Also the ironic tensions themselves can become the basis of a considerable body of war literature. The whole generation of novels of the absurd written not only in America but also in Europe in the late fifties depends on this very element.

One must also consider the way in which the younger generation in the western world as a whole sought to manufacture a set of heroes in the sixties. It has been noted that coverage of the battlefield by television and other media has helped to destroy popular belief in the hero-figure, especially insofar as the hero was traditionally a soldier. To counteract this tendency and help recreate the hero-figure in the national mind, one now sees the phenomenon of a younger generation that takes revolutinary figures—notably Che Guevara, Ho Chi Minh, and the Viet Cong in general—and carefully *avoids* examining either their methods or their motives too closely. George Woodcock made a comment that illustrates this point:

In the sixties Vietnam has given young radicals an issue on which to focus their rebellion. Not many of them have really thought out the issues of the war; certainly few have recognized that the Viet Cong are in fact totalitarian thugs who have forced the peasants of large areas into complicity by wholesale terror tactics. In consequence they compromise a legitimate opposition to the war as war by becoming partisans of one side, though the Viet Cong are less murderous than the Americans only because their material resources are less. But Vietnam is not a concrete reality to the New Left; it is a myth around which to crystallize personal and group discontents. No Mackenzie-Papineau Battalion has gone to help the Viet Cong. No Canadian students have died defending the Left in the jungles of the Mekong as their forerunners died beside the Ebro and the Jarama. There is no sixties equivalent of Norman Bethune. None has even felt the uneasy shame of staying at home while his friends have gone to Spain or its equivalent. By the same token, there has not been a disillusionment in Vietnam comparable to that which took place in Spain when foreign volunteers found how Stalinism had corrupted the side they supported. The New Leftists have never got near enough to "their side" in Vietnam to run the slightest risk of finding out disappointing truths.[22]

This desire to reestablish the hero as part of the national mythos could conceivably become the basis of a literature about the minor wars of the nuclear age.

An element of caution seems to be advisable when making predictions about the nature of the literature that will emerge from the war in Viet Nam. Observation of the pattern of past wars suggests that there is a gestation period of about ten years after the end of a given war before all of the most important novels are brought forth. For example, many critics writing in 1922 or 1923 made serious errors about the nature of World War I literature as a whole. A critic who would have tried to assess the novels of World War II in 1950 would have necessarily ignored *From Here to Eternity, Melville Goodwin, U.S.A., The Caine Mutiny,* and many others. It would be a brave or prescient critic who would attempt an overall analysis of the novels about the war in Viet Nam before 1980 at the earliest.

When the era of the world wars began, involving the United States willy-nilly in international affairs, nothing could have been more natural than that American authors deal with this great body of experience, just as the authors of the absurd acted characteristically in debunking a system that had proved unworkable. *Experience* is the key word here; the war novelists were writing not about a tradition but about current events. When the fund of experience was cut off by the threat of nuclear war, the writers necessarily turned to subtler reinterpretations of past events. Three of the more successful war novels written in the late sixties—Frederick Keefe's *The Investigating Officer* (1967), Anton Myrer's *Once an Eagle* (1968), and Alfred Coppel's *Order of Battle* (1968)—all return to the events of World War II for their story line.

The Investigating Officer is interesting both in the manner in which it reproduces some of the traditional aspects of the American war novel and in the new directions it indicates. It deals with two days in 1945 just after V-E Day when a newly arrived rear echelon officer is directed to investigate the circumstances surrounding the shooting of two German prisoners of war by an American lieutenant. The novel conforms to the traditional American pattern in that all the officers, even of this highly trained combat division, have come from civilian life. Also the familiar figure of the "interpreter" reappears in the person of Lieutenant Holly, an intellectual from the Army Historical Section who happens to be attached to the division when the investigation takes place. Like Sidney Skelton in *Melville Goodwin,* he understands the army mentality and explains it to the essentially civilian investigating officer.

The Investigating Officer diverges from the traditional American pattern in that it moves away from the procedural determinism that rendered many World War II novels indistinguishable from each other. Too often the novels about the Second World War were variations on *The Naked and the Dead* in which the individual was caught up in a vast and uncontrollable system, both military and social. Here the novelist turns toward an emphasis on individual thought and volition as a factor in conjunction with or in reaction against an apparent determinism, a reemphasizing of human responsibility. The investigating officer's real preoccupation is with the questions of how to act impartially, how to be fair when it would be better to be unfair, how to act significantly. He is also faced with the problem of dealing with the division's combat-hardened officers and their difficulty in adjusting to a peacetime morality after being totally involved in the war.

Interest in war literature will probably enjoy a new resurgence when the current spate of pacifism has passed. In *Waiting for the End* Fiedler claims that the pacifism of the sixties is only part of a pattern: each war is followed by such a movement.[23] His contention is supported by the evidence of the "Klingberg cycle," which suggests that "the shift in opinion on foreign policy in the mid-1960's appears to be simply the latest manifestation of a regular alternation in American attitudes toward foreign affairs between introversion and extraversion."[24] According to the Klingberg theory, the shift from extraversion to introversion should have begun to occur sometime in 1967; the prediction is accurate enough if one considers that anti–Viet Nam sentiment in general became increasingly important about that time. Possibly, therefore, the extreme pessimism characteristic of some works written in the sixties (such as Joseph Heller's play *We Bombed in New Haven*) may be superseded by a type of novel resembling those written by Crane and Melville in the nineteenth century—i.e., a novel in which war is treated objectively, as an interesting but not necessarily horrifying phenomenon. The climate of opinion is, after all, quite similar to that of the nineteenth century in this respect: in both cases writers are capable of writing about the effects a world war might have but are not really able to treat such a disaster as imminent; therefore, the tendency is to treat the subject of warfare in slightly idealized or theoretical terms.

Whatever new direction the war novel may take in the United States, it seems safe to predict its continuing importance and popularity. The theme of "men in arms" itself is indestructible, and the events of our time revolve as never before around the questions of peace and war. In such a situation one may subscribe to Joseph Remenyi's statement:

"[Great war literature] helps retain one's sense of value that ridicules absolute indifference or absolute futility. Man is shown as an agent of his own will, or as a puppet of forces which he could not control, . . . in his tireless integrity and in his selfish pettiness. . . . [It] touches the innermost existence of man, and defies the nothingness of human life with an . . . expression of actions and aims which are organically attached to the will to live and the will to die.[25]

WAR NOVELS REFERRED TO IN THE TEXT

Date given for foreign works is that of the English translation.

AUTHOR	TITLE	DATE
James Fenimore Cooper	*The Spy*	1821
John DeForest	*Miss Ravenel's Conversion*	1867
Herman Melville	*Billy Budd* written *c.* 1888, pub.	1924
Frank Stockton	*The Great War Syndicate*	1889
Ambrose Bierce	*Tales of Soldiers and Civilians*	1891
Stephen Crane	*The Red Badge of Courage*	1895
Mary R. S. Andrews	*Old Glory*	1917
Temple Bailey	*The Tin Soldier*	1918
Coningsby Dawson	*The Glory of the Trenches*	1918
Edward Streeter	*Dere Mable*	1918
Edith Wharton	*The Marne*	1918
Mary R. S. Andrews	*Joy in the Morning*	1919
John Dos Passos	*One Man's Initiation*	1920
John Dos Passos	*Three Soldiers*	1921
Willa Cather	*One of Ours*	1922
E. E. Cummings	*The Enormous Room*	1922
Edith Wharton	*A Son at the Front*	1923
Thomas Boyd	*Through the Wheat*	1923
Ernest Hemingway	*In Our Time*	1925
Henri Barbusse	*Under Fire*	1926
William Faulkner	*Soldiers' Pay*	1926
James Stevens	*Mattock*	1927
Arnold Zweig	*The Case of Sergeant Grischa*	1928
"Charles Edmonds"	*A Subaltern's War*	1929
Robert Graves	*Goodbye to All That*	1929
Ernest Hemingway	*A Farewell to Arms*	1929
Ernst Juenger	*Storm of Steel*	1929
Eva Maria Remarque	*All Quiet on the Western Front*	1929
Edmund Blunden	*Undertones of War*	1930
Jaroslav Hasek	*The Good Soldier Schweik*	1930
John Dos Passos	*1919*	1932
David Jones	*In Parenthesis*	1937
Dalton Trumbo	*Johnny Got His Gun*	1939

AUTHOR	TITLE	DATE
Ernest Hemingway	*For Whom the Bell Tolls*	1940
John Hersey	*Into the Valley*	1943
John Marquand	*So Little Time*	1943
Saul Bellow	*Dangling Man*	1944
Harry Brown	*A Walk in the Sun*	1944
John Hersey	*A Bell for Adano*	1944
Merle Miller	*That Winter*	1945
Robert Lowry	*Casualty*	1946
Thomas Heggen	*Mister Roberts*	1946
William Haines	*Command Decision*	1947
Allen Matthews	*Assault*	1947
James Michener	*Tales of the South Pacific*	1947
John Horne Burns	*The Gallery*	1948
James Gould Cozzens	*Guard of Honor*	1948
Martha Gellhorn	*The Wine of Astonishment*	1948
Norman Mailer	*The Naked and the Dead*	1948
Irwin Shaw	*The Young Lions*	1948
Heinrich Böll	*The Train Was on Time*	1949
Robert Bowen	*The Weight of the Cross*	1951
Egon Hostovsky	*The Lonely Rebels*	1951
James Jones	*From Here to Eternity*	1951
John Marquand	*Melville Goodwin, U.S.A.*	1951
Herman Wouk	*The Caine Mutiny*	1951
Pat Frank	*Hold Back the Night*	1952
James Michener	*The Bridges at Toko-ri*	1952
William Styron	*The Long March*	1953
Leon Uris	*Battle Cry*	1953
Pierre Boulle	*The Bridge on the River Kwai*	1954
William B. Huie	*The Execution of Private Slovik*	1954
Philip Wylie	*Tomorrow!*	1954
Ivan Bahrianyi	*The Hunters and the Hunted*	1955
"Peter Bamm"	*The Invisible Flag*	1956
Helmut Kirst	*Forward, Gunner Asch*	1956
Karl-Ludwig Opitz	*The General*	1956
"Friedrich Deich"	*The Sanity Inspectors*	1957
Mark Harris	*Something about a Soldier*	1957
"Sven Hassel"	*The Legion of the Damned*	1957
Theodore Plivier	*Stalingrad*	1957
John Hersey	*The War Lover*	1959
Joseph Heller	*Catch-22*	1961
Kurt Vonnegut	*Mother Night*	1961
Eugene Burdick and Harvey Wheeler	*Fail-Safe*	1962
James Jones	*The Thin Red Line*	1962
Fletcher Knebel and Charles W. Bailey	*Seven Days in May*	1962
Frederick Keefe	*The Investigating Officer*	1967

NOTES

PREFACE

1. Arthur M. Schlesinger, Jr., *A Thousand Days,* p. 275.
2. Ulysses S. Grant, *Personal Memoirs,* p. 22.
3. Arnold Toynbee, "The Changes in the United States Position and Outlook as a World Power During the Last Half-Century," in *Man, Science, Learning and Education,* ed. S. W. Higginbotham, pp. 16–17.
4. This point is discussed fully in C. Vann Woodward, "The Age of Reinterpretation," *American Historical Review,* LXVI, 1–19; and in Reinhold Niebuhr, *The Irony of American History,* pp. 38–39. To Niebuhr the United States' post-World War II commitment to international peacekeeping, coupled with its possession of the bomb, is the ultimate irony of American history.
5. Daniel Boorstin, *The Americans,* p. 375.
6. Norman Mailer, "Some Children of the Goddess," *Esquire,* LX, 65.

INTRODUCTION: 1880–1917

1. Marcus Cunliffe, *George Washington, Man and Monument,* p. 97.
2. Russell Weigley, *Towards an American Army,* pp. 6–7. Weigley also notes that the Americans made a deliberate attempt to pick off the enemy officers, contrary to the custom then prevailing in Europe.
3. Samuel P. Huntington, *The Soldier and the State,* pp. 198–99.
4. Julius W. Pratt, "The Business Attitude toward the Spanish-American War," in *Understanding the American Past,* ed. Edward N. Saveth, p. 421.
5. Ibid., pp. 418–19.
6. Theodore Roosevelt, *Atlantic,* LXVI, 567.
7. Joseph Heller, *Catch-22,* pp. 264–66.
8. Henry Adams, *A History of the United States of America,* IX, 228.
9. Robert Sherwood, *Roosevelt and Hopkins,* pp. 39–40.
10. Dorothy Goebel and Julius Goebel, *Generals in the White House,* p. 17.
11. Nonetheless, even the coach must cooperate with the administration. As Samuel P. Huntington has pointed out, "That officer has . . . generally been unsuccessful who has attempted to vindicate himself at the polls for rough treatment accorded him while in the service by a hostile administration" (p. 160). The Americans want a winner, but they know that a prima donna means trouble and shy away from him.
12. James Jones, *The Thin Red Line,* pp. 182–83.
13. Alexis de Tocqueville, *Democracy in America,* p. 528.
14. Alfred Vagts, *A History of Militarism, Civilian and Military,* p. 98. See also T. Harry Williams, *Americans at War,* pp. 1–43.

15. Vagts, p. 101.
16. Harry S. Truman, *Memoirs*, I, 128.
17. Robert A. Lively, *Fiction Fights the Civil War*, pp. 44–45.
18. Henry O. Dwight, "How We Fight at Atlanta," *Harper's*, XXIX, 648.
19. Daniel McCook, "The Second Division at Shiloh," *Harper's*, XXVIII, 831.
20. Walter Millis, *Arms and Men*, p. 175.
21. Huntington, p. 151.
22. V. S. Pritchett, "American Soldiers," *New Statesman*, LXV, 207.
23. Adams, p. 220.
24. Millis, p. 190.
25. Roosevelt, p. 567.
26. Harold Sprout and Margaret Sprout, *The Rise of American Naval Power, 1776–1918*, p. 309.
27. Quoted in Frederic René Coudert, *A Half Century of International Problems*, p. 219.
28. Benedetto Croce, *My Philosophy and Other Essays*, p. 120.
29. Millis, p. 135.
30. Or on military discipline for that matter. When the *Billy Budd* theme was played out in real life in the case of Private Eddie Slovik in 1945, the reasons for Slovik's execution were far removed from the harsh but honorable conduct of Captain Vere.
31. Hennig Cohen, ed., *Selected Poems of Herman Melville*, p. 17.
32. There is also some suggestion that *Billy Budd* represents a certain exoneration of the conduct of Melville's cousin Guert Gansevoort, who had been presiding officer in the *Somers* mutiny trial in 1841. Gansevoort had apparently allowed himself to be pressured by the ship's captain into finding against the defendants—the son of the Secretary of War and two ordinary seamen. One of the seamen, Elisha Small, cried out, "God bless the flag!" as he was hanged, from which an obvious parallel can be drawn with Billy's last words, especially as Small is popularly supposed to have been innocent (Leon Howard, *Herman Melville, a Biography*, pp. 324–27). See also Marcus Cunliffe, *Soldiers and Civilians*, pp. 96–97; and Harrison Hayford, ed., *The Somers Mutiny Affair*, passim.
33. Ambrose Bierce, *In the Midst of Life and Other Stories*, p. 98.
34. Ibid., p. 79.
35. Samuel Flagg Bemis, "The Shifting Strategy of American Defense and Diplomacy," in *Essays in History and International Relations*, p. 5.
36. Julius W. Pratt, "The 'Large Policy' of 1898," in *Recent America*, p. 20.
37. Sprout and Sprout, pp. 215–16.
38. Millis, p. 158, my italics.
39. Huntington, pp. 266–68.
40. Luther L. Bernard, *War and Its Causes*, pp. 251–54.
41. Richard W. Van Alstyne, *American Diplomacy in Action*, p. 254. W. R. Brock also comments on the element of idealism in American foreign policy in *The Character of American History*, pp. 200–202. Richard Hofstadter provides further evidence of the nonrational basis of American expansion in the late nineteenth century in "Manifest Destiny and the Philippines," in *Crisis in America*, pp. 175–82. A detailed account of the steps leading up to the war with Spain is available in Ernest R. May, *Imperial Democracy*, pp. 131–48.
42. Bernard, chs. 13–16.

PART ONE: 1917–1939

1. THE CRUSADE

1. "War's Reaction on Literature," *Nation*, XCIX, 765.
2. H. C. Peterson, *Propaganda for War*, p. 5.
3. Walter Millis, *Road to War*, p. 48.
4. Robert L. Bullard, *Personalities and Reminiscences of the War*, pp. 82–83.
5. John Dos Passos, *Three Soldiers*, pp. 213–14.
6. Willia Cather, *One of Ours*, p. 458.
7. Edith Wharton, *A Son at the Front*, p. 166.
8. Cather, p. 257.
9. Ibid., p. 244.
10. Ibid., p. 274.
11. Ibid., p. 375.
12. Charles A. Fenton, "A Literary Fracture of World War I," *American Quarterly*, XII, 119–32.
13. Ibid.
14. E. E. Cummings, *The Enormous Room*, p. 23.
15. Cather, p. 284.
16. Charles A. Fenton, "Ambulance Drivers in France and Italy," *American Quarterly*, III, 326–42.
17. Archibald MacLeish, "Lines for an Interment," *New Republic*, LXXVI, 159.
18. Millis, p. 68.
19. Eugene Löhrke, *Armageddon*, p. 3.
20. Cather, p. 327.
21. Ibid., pp. 167–68.

2. PROTEST

1. E. E. Cummings, *The Enormous Room*, p. 199.
2. Robert L. Bullard, *Personalities and Reminiscences of the War*, p. 267.
3. Clennell Wilkinson, "Back to All That," *London Mercury*, XXII, 540.
4. Some statistics: The Marne: 500,000 casualties on each side; Verdun: 362,000 Allied casualties, 336,000 German; The Somme: 614,000 Allies, 650,000 Germans; Third Ypres: 370,000 British casualties (Theodore Ropp, *War in the Western World*, pp. 23–31).
5. Leonard P. Ayres, *The War with Germany*, p. 119.
6. Ernest Hemingway, *A Farewell to Arms*, p. 137.
7. Edith Wharton, *A Son at the Front*, p. 165.
8. Thomas Boyd, *Through the Wheat*, p. 215.
9. James Stevens, *Mattock*, p. 282.
10. Cummings, p. 198.
11. Hemingway, p. 48.
12. Cummings, p .192.
13. Willa Cather, *One of Ours*, p. 358.
14. Dixon Wecter, *When Johnny Comes Marching Home*, p. 470.
14. Hemingway, pp. 174–75.
16. Hemingway, *In Our Time*, p. 82.

17. Quoted in Stanley Cooperman, *World War I and the American Novel*, p. 109.
18. Hemingway, *Farewell to Arms*, p. 137.
19. Wharton, p. 239.
20. Ibid., p. 265.
21. Boyd, p. 266.
22. Malcolm Cowley, *Exile's Return*, p. 38.

3. THE WAR AS METAPHOR

1. Eugene Löhrke, *Armageddon*, p. 3.
2. James D. Hart, *The Popular Book*, p. 226.
3. Helen McAfee, "The Literature of Disillusion," *Atlantic Monthly*, CXXXII, 228–29.
4. John W. Aldridge, *After the Lost Generation*, p. 5.
5. Charles A. Fenton, "Ambulance Drivers in France and Italy," *American Quarterly*, III, 342.
6. Vernon Parrington, *The Beginnings of Critical Realism in America*, III, 412.
7. Frederick S. Hoffman, *The Twenties*, p. 75.
8. Joseph Warren Beach, *American Fiction, 1920–1940*, p. 351.
9. Milton Rugoff, "Dos Passos, Novelist of Our Time," *Sewanee Review*, XLIX, 454.
10. Alfred Kazin, *On Native Grounds*, p. 325.
11. E. E. Cummings, *The Enormous Room*, p. 181.
12. Alan Calmer, "John Dos Passos," *Sewanee Review*, XL, 341.
13. Cummings, p. 293.
14. Edmund Wilson, *The Shores of Light*, p. 99.
15. John Dos Passos, *Three Soldiers*, p. 96.
16. Ibid., p. 82.
17. Ernest Hemingway, *A Farewell to Arms*, p. 125.
18. William Faulkner, *Soldiers' Pay*, p. 173.
19. Wilson, p. 101.

4. EUROPEAN CONTEMPORARIES

1. Edith Wharton, *A Son at the Front*, p. 165.
2. Robert Graves, *Goodbye to All That*, p. 121.
3. Ibid., p. 122.
4. Charles Edmonds, *A Subaltern's War*, p. 14.
5. Ernst Juenger, *Storm of Steel*, p. 314.
6. Clennell Wilkinson, "Recent War Books," *London Mercury*, XXI, 236.
7. Arnold Zweig, *The Case of Sergeant Grischa*, p. 170.
8. Robert L. Bullard, *Personalities and Reminiscences of the War*, p. 240.
9. Malcolm Cowley, "John Dos Passos: The Poet and the World," *New Republic*, LXX, 303.
10. John Dos Passos, *Three Soldiers*, p. 231.
11. Eugene Löhrke, *Armageddon*, p. 18.
12. Edmund Blunden, *Undertones of War*, p. 129.
13. Edmonds, p. 14.

5. THE THIRTIES

1. André Maurois, *The New Freedom to the New Frontier,* p. 122.
2. Bernard De Voto, *Literary Fallacy,* pp. 167–69.
3. Malcolm Cowley, *The Literary Situation,* p. 37.
4. Mark Van Doren, "Post-War: The Literary Twenties," *Harper's* CLXXIII, 240.
5. Philip Rahv, "In Retrospect," in *Partisan Review Anthology,* eds. William Phillips and Philip Rahv, p. 682.
6. Edmund Wilson, *The Shores of Light,* pp. 498–99.
7. Ernest Hemingway, *For Whom the Bell Tolls,* pp. 467–68.
8. Ibid., p. 328.
9. Allen Guttman, *The Wound in the Heart,* pp. 192–95.
10. Stanley Cooperman, *World War I and the American Novel,* p. 84.
11. Robert E. Sherwood, *Roosevelt and Hopkins,* pp. 380–81.

PART TWO: 1939–1952

6. INTRODUCTION

1. Samuel P. Huntington, *The Soldier and the State,* pp. 222–23.
2. Dorothy B. Goebel, *American Foreign Policy,* p. 259.
3. Social Service Research Council, *Civil-Military Relations,* p. viii.
4. The strength of the U.S. Army (including the Air Force) at the end of June 1940 was 267,767 men; the Navy had 160,997 (David A. Shannon, *Between the Wars,* p. 223).
5. Manfred Jonas, *Isolationism in America, 1935–1941,* pp. 27–28.
6. Samuel E. Morison, *The Oxford History of the American People,* p. 991.
7. Wayne S. Cole, *Senator Gerald P. Nye and American Foreign Relations,* pp. 66–67.
8. Ibid., p. 80.
9. Allen Guttman, *The Wound in the Heart,* p. 192.
10. Hugh Thomas, *The Spanish Civil War,* p. 797.
11. The Abraham Lincoln Battalion had casualties of 66% of the troops engaged at its first battle on the Jarama in February 1937 (Richard P. Traina, *American Diplomacy and the Spanish Civil War,* p. 172). Of the 2,800 Americans who fought in Spain, 900 were killed (Thomas, p. 797).
12. Jonas, p. 25.
13. Goebel, p. 277.
14. Alexander De Conde, ed., *Isolation and Security,* p. 58.
15. Goebel, p. 281.
16. For example, the speeches made by James Bryan Conant, President of Harvard University, 21 October, 1940; Harold L. Ickes, Secretary of the Interior, 18 May, 1941; Frank Knox, Secretary of the Navy, 15 September, 1941; Dorothy Thompson, journalist, 2 May, 1941. Speeches by other leaders like Charles Lindbergh and Norman Thomas deplored this fact but thereby acknowledged it (Lewis Copeland, ed., *The World's Great Speeches,* pp. 558 ff.).
17. See Stephen Vincent Benét, ed., *Zero Hour,* passim.

18. Goebel, p. 287.
19. Robert E. Sherwood, *Roosevelt and Hopkins,* p. 128.
20. Malcolm Cowley, "War Novels: After Two Wars," in *Modern American Fiction,* ed. A. Walton Litz, p. 300.
21. John Aldridge, "The New Generation of Writers," *Harper's,* CXXXIV, 424.
22. H. Zentner, "Morale," *American Sociological Review,* XVI, 301.
23. Gerald W. Johnson, *Incredible Tale,* p. 228.
24. V. S. Pritchett, "American Soldiers," *New Statesman,* LXV, 207.
25. Cowley, p. 301.

7. THE CIVILIAN SOLDIER

1. Edith Wharton, *A Son at the Front,* p. 114.
2. William Bradford Huie, *The Execution of Private Slovik,* p. 13.
3. Robert E. Sherwood, *Roosevelt and Hopkins,* p. 560.
4. Norman Mailer, *The Naked and the Dead,* p. 59.
5. Ibid., p. 69.
6. Saul Bellow, *Dangling Man,* p. 139.
7. Ibid., p. 138.
8. Robert Lowry, *Casualty,* p. 143.
9. Bernard Berelson and Morris Janowitz, eds., *A Reader in Public Opinion and Communications,* pp. 281–82.
10. James Gould Cozzens, *Guard of Honor,* pp. 275–76.
11. Ernie Pyle, *Here Is Your War,* pp. 306 ff.
12. Joseph Heller, *Catch-22,* p. 91.
13. Ibid.
14. Thomas Heggen, *Mr. Roberts,* p. xii.
15. William Styron, *The Long March,* p. 36.
16. Ibid., p. 51.
17. Yeats, William Butler. "An Irish Airman Foresees His Death," *The Collected Poems,* p. 152.
18. M. R. Kadish, *Point of Honor,* Toronto, 1951, quoted in Malcolm Cowley, *The Literary Situation,* p. 39.
19. Alfred Hayes, *The Girl on the Via Flaminia,* p. 164.

8. THE PROFESSIONAL OFFICER

1. C. Wright Mills, *The Power Elite,* p. 173 .
2. Norman Mailer, *The Naked and the Dead,* p. 425.
3. Ibid., p. 428.
4. Morris Janowitz, *The Professional Soldier,* p. 21.
5. The excellence of many films based on war novels and the increasing importance of the film medium as an extension of the novel suggest that it is reasonable to make at least passing reference to them in any study of the novel itself.
6. John Marquand, *Melville Goodwin, U.S.A.,* p. 594.
7. Ibid., p. 113.
8. William Bradford Huie, *The Execution of Private Slovik,* p. 76.
9. Ibid., p. 75.
10. Norman Podhoretz, *Doings and Undoings,* pp. 181–86.
11. Herman Wouk, *The Caine Mutiny,* p. 361.
12. Irwin Shaw, *The Young Lions,* p. 463.
13. Ibid., p. 549.

9. THE JEW IN THE AMERICAN WAR NOVEL

1. Alfred Kazin, "The Jew as Modern American Writer," in *Commentary Reader*, pp. xxi–xxii.
2. Saul Bellow, *Dangling Man*, p. 53.
3. Ibid., p. 52.
4. Ibid., p. 55.
5. Ibid., p. 69.
6. Robert Sherwood, *Roosevelt and Hopkins*, p. 167.
7. Norman Mailer, *The Naked and the Dead*, p. 562.
8. Alfred Kazin, "The Mindless Young Militants," *Commentary*, VI, 499–501.

10. ASSESSMENT

1. Albert Van Nostrand, *The Denatured Novel*, p. 183.
2. Alfred Kazin, "The Mindless Young Militants," *Commentary*, VI, 496.
3. C. B. MacDonald, "Novels of World War II," *Military Affairs*, XIII, 43.
4. John Horne Burns, *The Gallery*, p. 157.
5: Ernest Jones, *Essays in Applied Psychoanalysis*, p. 70.
6. Ernest Hemingway, *A Farewell to Arms*, p. 54.
7. Van Nostrand, pp. 179–83.
8. Joseph Remenyi, "The Psychology of War Literature," *Sewanee Review*, LII, 137.
9. Malcolm Cowley, "War Novels: After Two Wars," in *Modern American Fiction*, ed. A. Walton Litz, p. 309.
10. Leslie Fiedler, "The Ant and the Grasshopper," *Partisan Review*, XXII, 412.
11. John Aldridge, *After the Lost Generation*, p. 89.
12. Van Nostrand, pp. 183, 188.
13. Philip Rahv, "The Cult of Experience in American Writing," *Partisan Review*, VII, 412–24.
14. William Phillips, "What Happened in the Thirties," in *Commentary Reader*, ed. Norman Podhoretz, p. 762.
15. Amy Loveman, "Then and Now," *Saturday Review of Literature*, XXVII, 8.
16. John McCormick, *Catastrophe and Imagination*, p. 221.
17. Cowley, pp. 311–12.
18. Aldridge, pp. 114–15.
19. Norman Podhoretz, *Doings and Undoings*, pp. 183–84.
20. Fiedler, *Waiting for the End*, p. 30.

11. KOREA

1. Arthur Schlesinger, *A Thousand Days*, p. 307.
2. William Styron, *The Long March*, p. 9.
3. Joseph Heller, *Catch-22*, p. 455.
4. Morris Janowitz, *The Professional Soldier*, p. 440.
5. Styron, p. 27.
6. James Michener, *The Bridges at Toko-ri*, p. 42.
7. Pat Frank, *Hold Back the Night*, p. 63.

PART THREE: 1953–1963

12. BLURRING OF DISTINCTION BETWEEN
CIVILIAN AND MILITARY ORGANIZATIONS

1. Samuel P. Huntington, *The Soldier and the State*, p. 345.
2. Stanley Uys, "[Senator Robert F.] Kennedy Angers Regime," *Montreal Star*, 13 June, 1966, p. 10.
3. Vannevar Bush, *Endless Horizons*, pp. 86–92.
4. Morris Janowitz, "Military Elites and the Study of War," in *War*, eds. Leon Bramson and G. Goethals, p. 343.
5. These and many other terms are defined in D. M. Abshire and R. V. Allen, eds., *National Security*, a good single-volume source of nuclear strategic jargon. The plot of *Fail-Safe* is based on a "barely nuclear war" and also illustrates the "nth country problem."
6. Abshire and Allen, p. 472.
7. Samuel P. Huntington, *Changing Patterns of Military Politics*. pp. 13–14.
8. "The Two Presidents," *Nation*, CCVIII, 778.
9. Henry Brandon, "The Unwinnable War," *Sunday Times*, London, 13 April, 1969, p. 50.
10. Edmond L. Volpe, "James Jones—Norman Mailer," in *Contemporary American Novelists*, ed. Harry T. Moore, p. 107.
11. John McCormick, *Catastrophe and Imagination*, p. 222.
12. Those critics who have dealt with Spillane's work emphasize the fact that Mike Hammer is a hero who responds to a profound need on the part of the American reading public. In an article that is not entirely facetious, Charles J. Rolo claims that Spillane's works are modern versions of the medieval Morality play and that Hammer is "the Superman [who] fights our fight against the forces of evil" ("Simenon and Spillane: The Metaphysics of Murder for Millions," in *New World Writing*, pp. 234–45). On the other hand, Christopher La Farge saw Hammer as a reincarnation of the Vigilante, a man who would deal with the spectre of Communism that had been raised by Senator Joseph McCarthy ("Mickey Spillane and His Bloody Hammer," *Saturday Review*, XXXVII, 12).
13. George Grella, "James Bond, Culture Hero," *New Republic*, CL, 17.
14. Grella's article is in many ways more interesting than the novels themselves. He points out that the catalog of Bond's possessions—Walther pistol, Bentley car, Sea Island cotton shirts—parallels similar detailed descriptions of the possessions of heroes like Achilles. Like Ulysses, Bond travels to exotic regions and even visits the underworld (the sewers of Istanbul or Dr. No's tunnel of terror); like St. George or Perseus he braves a fiery monster to save a maiden (in *The Moonraker*). Many other critics (including Kingsley Amis, "Literary Agents," *New Statesman*, LXVII, 452–53; and Malcolm Muggeridge, "James Bond: The Myth and Its Master," *Observer*, 30 May, 1965, p. 21) have dealt with the James Bond phenomenon. Perhaps the last word was said by an Italian critic who accused Fleming of inventing "a mythical hero, possibly a folk hero extolling the Aryan race, within a socio-politico-geographical vacuum" (cited by Robert J. Clements in "The European Literary Scene," *Saturday Review*, XLVIII, 22).
15. Kurt Vonnegut, *Player Piano*, p. 216.

16. Theodore Sorensen, *Kennedy*, pp. 737–94.
17. Apparently not a real possibility under existing circumstances: "The so-called 'fail-safe' procedure . . . in essence precludes SAC planes from proceeding beyond a predetermined point without an explicit 'go' order, an order which must come from the highest authority and which cannot be triggered by some mechanical failure" (William Kaufman, *The McNamara Strategy*, p. 140).
18. Eugene Burdick and Harvey Wheeler, *Fail-Safe*, p. 134.
19. Ibid., p. 257.

13. THE ABSURD

1. Joseph J. Waldmeir, "Ideological Aspects of the American Novels of World War II," Ph.D. dissertation, pp. 181–91.
2. James M. Etheridge, ed., *Contemporary Authors*, VII–VIII, 238.
3. André Maurois, *Les discours du docteur O'Grady*, pp. 26–27.
4. V. S. Pritchett, "American Soldiers," *New Statesman*, LXV, 207.
5. John McCormick, *Catastrophe and Imagination*, p. 228.
6. Sidney Hook, et al., "Western Values and Total War," *Commentary*, XXXII, 278.
7. R. Ainsztein, "Soviet Russian War Novels since Stalin's Death," *Twentieth Century*, CLXVII, 328–38.
8. William Styron, "My Generation," *Esquire*, LXX, 123.
9. Samuel P. Huntington, "No More Viet Nams? A Symposium," *Atlantic*, CCXXII, 107.
10. Walter Millis, *Arms and Men*, p. 78.
11. James Gould Cozzens, *Guard of Honor*, p. 28.
12. James Jones, *The Thin Red Line*, p. 354.
13. Ibid., p. 130.
14. Huntington, *The Soldier and the State*, pp. 257–58.
15. Ibid., p. 281.

14. THE NONHERO

1. James Gould Cozzens, *Guard of Honor*, p. 358.
2. Arthur M. Schlesinger, Jr., *A Thousand Days*, p. 88.
3. William Styron, *The Long March*, p. 91.
4. Ibid., p. 38.
5. Malcolm Cowley, *The Literary Situation*, pp. 26–27.
6. Louis Smith, *American Democracy and Military Power*, p. 58.
7. Norman Podhoretz, *Doings and Undoings*, p. 209.
8. Vance Ramsey, "From Here to Absurdity: Heller's *Catch-22*" in *Seven Contemporary Authors*, ed. Thomas B. Whitbread, p. 103.
9. Richard P. Adams, "A Second Look at *From Here to Eternity*," *College English*, XVII, 208.
10. Mark Harris, *Something about a Soldier*, p. 58.
11. Randall Jarrell, *Selected Poems*, p. 197.
12. Harris, p. 58.
13. James Jones, *The Thin Red Line*, p. 388.
14. Sidney Hook, et al., "Western Values and Total War," *Commentary*, XXXII, 278.
15. R. H. Smith, "A Review: *Catch-22*," in *The American Reading Public*, ed. R. H. Smith, pp. 237–38.
16. Leslie Fiedler, *Waiting for the End*, p. 30.

17. Podhoretz, pp. 223–24.
18. Joseph Heller, *Catch-22*, p. 455.
19. Ibid., p. 461.
20. Frederick R. Karl, "Joseph Heller's *Catch-22*: Only Fools Walk in Darkness," in *Contemporary American Novelists*, ed. Harry T. Moore, p. 138.

15. BLACK HUMOR

1. William W. Kaufman, *The McNamara Strategy*, p. 36.
2. Kenneth W. Thompson, "Nuclear Weapons: Four Crucial Questions," in *Conflict and Cooperation among Nations*, ed. I. Duchacek, p. 447.
3. As was the speech made by Assistant Secretary of Defense John T. McNaughton on 19 December, 1962, in which he said that the key to avoiding panic-stricken use of nuclear weapons lies in "survivability": i.e., the assurance that the United States could survive any surprise attack and still have enough forces operational to deliver a controlled counterattack. Therefore, "a potential enemy need not fear the fears of the United States, and the United States need not fear that he fears its fears; so one side need not be under compulsion to attack the other whenever the situation becomes confused" (Kaufman, p. 142).
4. Herman Kahn, "Some Comments on Controlled War," in *The Debate over Thermonuclear Strategy*, ed. A. I. Waskow, Boston, 1965, pp. 18–29.
5. Lewis Copeland, ed., *The World's Great Speeches*, p. 637.
6. Richard B. Sewall, *The Vision of Tragedy*, pp. 81–82.
7. Daniel Lerner, *Sykewar*, pp. 202–5.
8. William Bittner, "Schweik among the Herrenvolk," *Nation*, CLXXXIV, 551.
9. Ernst Kris and Nathan Leites, "Trends in Twentieth Century Propaganda," in *Reader in Public Opinion and Communications*, eds. Bernard Berelson and Morris Janowitz, p. 283.
10. Kenneth Burke, "War, Response and Contradiction," in *The Philosophy of Literary Form*, p. 205.
11. Vance Ramsey, "From Here to Absurdity," in *Seven Contemporary Authors*, ed. Thomas B. Whitbread, p. 105.
12. Mark Harris, *Something about a Soldier*, p. 108.
13. Ibid., p. 109.
14. Joseph Heller, *Catch-22*, p. 449.
15. C. Vann Woodward, "The Age of Reinterpretation," *American Historical Review*, LXVI, 13.

16. THE WAR NOVEL AS POP ART

1. John Rublowsky, *Pop Art*, pp. 3–4.
2. Lucy R. Lippard, ed., *Pop Art*, pp. 9–10.
3. Ibid., p. 98.
4. James Jones, *The Thin Red Line*, p. 151.
5. Sanford Pinsker, "Heller's *Catch-22*: The Protest of a 'Puer Eternis,'" *Critique*, VII, 161.
6. Norman Mailer, "Some Children of the Goddess," *Esquire*, LX, 65.
7. Vance Ramsey, "From Here to Absurdity," in *Seven Contemporary Authors*, ed. Thomas B. Whitbread, p. 108.

8. Joseph Heller, *Catch-22*, pp. 147–48.
9. Donald Duncan, *The New Legions*, pp. 6–7.

17. CONCLUSION

1. George Santayana, *Character and Opinion in the United States*, p. 141.
2. Dorothy Goebel and Julius Goebel, *Generals in the White House*, p. 20.
3. Leslie Fiedler, *Waiting for the End*, p. 27.
4. William F. Nolan, "Thirty-six Books a Year Was Faust's Gift to the Pulps," *Montreal Star*, 6 Dec. 1969, p. 52.
5. E.g., Lewis Mumford in *The City in History*, and Nigel Calder in *The Environment Game*.
6. Lewis Mumford, *The Golden Day*, pp. 47–81.
7. John W. Muste, "Better to Die Laughing: The War Novels of Joseph Heller and John Ashmead," *Critique*, V, 17.
8. Saul Bellow, *Dangling Man*, p. 8.
9. James Baldwin, *The Fire Next Time*, p. 47.
10. Reinhold Niebuhr, *The Irony of American History*, p. 41.
11. Edmund L. Volpe, "James Jones—Norman Mailer" in *Contemporary American Novelists*, ed. Harry T. Moore, p. 108.
12. Ibid., p. 109.
13. Ralph W. Emerson, *Essays, First Series*, p. 14.
14. Daniel J. Boorstin, *The Americans*, p. 404.
15. Walter Millis, *Road to War*, p. 319.
16. Samuel P. Huntington, *The Soldier and the State*, p. 389.
17. Vance Packard, *The Pyramid Climbers*, p. 189.
18. Morris Janowitz, *The Professional Soldier*, pp. 224–26.
19. Don Wakefield, "Supernation at Peace and War," *Atlantic*, CCXXI, 95.
20. E. S. Turner, "Boy, Did We Clobber the Mahrattas!" *Punch*, CCLIV, 337–38.
21. Bernard Bergonzi, *Heroes' Twilight*, p. 180.
22. George Woodcock, "The Thirties and the Sixties," *Saturday Night*, LXXXIV, 37.
23. Fiedler, p. 27.
24. Cited by Samuel P. Huntington in "No More Viet Nams? A Symposium," *Atlantic*, CCXXII, 107.
25. Joseph Remenyi, "The Psychology of War Literature," *Sewanee Review*, LII, 147.

SELECTED BIBLIOGRAPHY

Aaron, Daniel, ed. *America in Crisis*. New York, 1952.

Abshire, D. M., and R. V. Allen, eds. *National Security: Political, Military and Economic Strategies in the Decade Ahead*. New York, 1963.

Adams, Henry. *A History of the United States of America during the Administrations of Jefferson and Madison*. New York, 1889–91; repub. 1962.

Adams, Richard P. "A Second Look at *From Here to Eternity*," *College English*, XVII (Jan. 1956), 205–10.

Ainsztein, R. "Soviet Russian War Novels since Stalin's Death," *Twentieth Century*, CLXVII (Apr. 1960), 328–38.

Aldridge, John. *After the Lost Generation*. New York, 1951.

———. "The New Generation of Writers," *Harper's*, CXXXIV (1947), 423–32.

Amis, Kingsley. "Literary Agents," *New Statesman*, LXVII (30 Mar., 1964), 452–53.

Ayres, Leonard P. *The War with Germany: A Statistical Summary*. Washington, 1919.

Bahrianyi, Ivan. *The Hunters and the Hunted*, trans. George S. N. Luckyj. Toronto, 1955.

Bailey, Charles W., and Fletcher Knebel. *Seven Days in May*. New York, 1962.

Baldwin, Hanson W. "When the Big Guns Speak," in *Public Opinion and Foreign Policy*, ed. Lester Markel, et al. New York, 1949, pp. 97–120.

Baldwin, James. *The Fire Next Time*. Harmondsworth, 1964.

"Bamm, Peter," pseud. of Kurt Emmrich. *The Invisible Flag*, trans. Frank Herman. New York, 1956.

Barbusse, Henri. *Under Fire*, trans. W. Fitzwater Wray. London, 1926.

Beach, Joseph Warren. *American Fiction, 1920–1940*. New York, 1941.

Bellow, Saul. *Dangling Man*. Harmondsworth, 1968.

Bemis, Samuel Flagg. "The Shifting Strategy of American Defense and Diplomacy," in *Essays in History and International Relations, in Honor of G. H. Blakeslee*. Worcester, Mass., 1949.

Benét, Stephen Vincent, ed. *Zero Hour: A Summons to the Free*. New York, 1940.

Berelson, Bernard, and Morris Janowitz, eds. *Reader in Public Opinion and Communications*, enl. ed. Glencoe, Ill. 1953.

Bergonzi, Bernard. *Heroes' Twilight: A Study of the Literature of the Great War*. London, 1965.

Bernard, Luther L. *War and Its Causes*. New York, 1944.

Bierce, Ambrose. *In the Midst of Life and Other Tales*. New York, 1961.

Billington, Ray Allen. "Middle Western Isolationism," in *Understanding the American Past*, ed. Edward N. Saveth. Boston, 1954, pp. 451–71.

Bittner, William. "Schweik among the Herrenvolk," *Nation*, CLXXXIV (22 June, 1957), 550–52.

Blunden, Edmund. *Undertones of War*. London, 1930.

Böll, Heinrich. *The Train Was on Time*, trans. Richard Graves. London, 1967.

"Boom to Bust," *Time*, LXXIX (18 May, 1962), 20.

Boorstin, Daniel J. *The Americans: The Colonial Experience*. Harmondsworth, 1965.

Boulle, Pierre. *The Bridge on the River Kwai*, trans. Xan Fielding. London, 1954.

Bourne, Randolph. *History of a Literary Radical, and Other Essays*. New York, 1920.

Bowen, Robert. *The Weight of the Cross*. New York, 1951.

Boyd, Thomas. *Through the Wheat*. New York, 1923.

Brock, Peter. *Pacifism in the United States from the Colonial Era to the First World War*. Princeton, 1968.

Brock, W. R. *The Character of American History*. London, 1960.

Brown, Harry. *A Walk in the Sun*. New York, 1944.

Bullard, Robert L. *Personalities and Reminiscences of the War*. New York, 1925.

Burdick, Eugene, and Harvey Wheeler. *Fail-Safe*. New York, 1962.

Burke, Kenneth. "War, Response and Contradiction," in *The Philosophy of Literary Form*. New York, 1957.

Burns, John Horne. *The Gallery*. London, 1964.

Bush, Vannevar. *Endless Horizons*. Washington, 1946.

Calder, Nigel. *The Environment Game*. London, 1969.

Calmer, Alan. "John Dos Passos," *Sewanee Review*, XL (1932), 341–49.

Calmer, Ned. *The Strange Land*. New York, 1950.

Cather, Willa. *One of Ours*. New York, 1922.

Clements, Robert J. "The European Literary Scene," *Saturday Review*, XLVIII (7 Aug., 1965), 21–22.

Cohen, Hennig, ed. *Selected Poems of Herman Melville*. New York, 1946.

Cole, Wayne S. *Senator Gerald P. Nye and American Foreign Relations*. Minneapolis, 1962.

Conroy, Frank. "My Generation," *Esquire*, LXX (Oct. 1968), 124–26.

Cooperman, Stanley. *World War I and the American Novel*. Baltimore, 1967.

Copeland, Lewis, ed. *The World's Great Speeches*, 2nd rev. ed. New York, 1958.

Coudert, Frederic René. *A Half Century of International Problems*. New York, 1954.

Cowley, Malcolm. *Exile's Return*. New York, 1956.

———. "John Dos Passos: The Poet and the World," *New Republic*, LXX (27 April, 1932), 303–5.

———. *The Literary Situation*. New York, 1954.

———. "War Novels: After Two Wars," in *Modern American Fiction*, ed. A. Walton Litz. Oxford, 1963, pp. 296–314.

Cozzens, James Gould. *Guard of Honor*. New York, 1948.

Crane, Stephen. *The Red Badge of Courage*. New York, 1952.

Croce, Benedetto. *My Philosophy and Other Essays*. New York, 1949.

Cummings, E. E. *The Enormous Room*. New York, 1922.

Cunliffe, Marcus. *George Washington, Man and Monument*. New York, 1960.

———. *Soldiers and Civilians*. Boston, 1968.

Davidson, David. *The Steeper Cliff*. New York, 1947.

DeConde, Alexander, ed. *Isolation and Security*. Durham, N.C., 1957.

"Deich, Friedrich," pseud. of F. A. Weeren. *The Sanity Inspectors,* trans. Robert Kee. New York, 1957.

De Voto, Bernard. *Literary Fallacy.* New York, 1944.

Donovan, Robert J. *Eisenhower: The Inside Story.* New York, 1956.

Dos Passos, John. *1919.* New York, 1932.

———. *Three Soldiers.* New York, 1921.

Duncan, Donald. *The New Legions.* New York, 1967.

Dwight, Henry O. "How We Fight at Atlanta," *Harper's,* XXIX (Oct. 1864), 648–49.

"Edmonds, Charles," pseud. *A Subaltern's War.* London, 1929; reprinted 1964.

Ekirch, A. A. *The Civilian and the Military.* New York, 1956.

Emerson, Ralph W. *Essays, First Series.* London, n.d.

Etheridge, James M., ed. *Contemporary Authors,* 20 vols. Detroit, 1962–.

Faulkner, William. *Soldiers' Pay.* New York, 1926.

Fenton, Charles A. "Ambulance Drivers in France and Italy: 1914–1918," *American Quarterly,* III (1951), 326–42.

———. "A Literary Fracture of World War I," *American Quarterly,* XII (Summer 1960), 119–32.

Fiedler, Leslie. "The Ant and the Grasshopper," review of *The Twenties: American Writing in the Post-War Decade* by Frederick J. Hoffman. *Partisan Review,* XXII (Summer 1955), 412–17.

———. *Waiting for the End.* London, 1965.

Fitzgerald, F. Scott. *The Great Gatsby.* New York, 1925.

Frank, Pat. *Hold Back the Night.* New York, 1952.

Frederick, Pierce G. *The Great Adventure: America in the First World War.* Indianapolis, 1961.

Frohock, W. M. *The Novel of Violence in America.* Dallas, 1958.

Galbraith, J. K. *The Great Crash, 1929.* Harmondsworth, 1968.

Gellhorn, Martha. *The Wine of Astonishment.* New York, 1948.

Goebel, Dorothy B. *American Foreign Policy: A Documentary Survey, 1776–1960,* New York, 1961.

Goebel, Dorothy and Julius Goebel. *Generals in the White House.* New York, 1945.

Grant, Ulysses S. *Personal Memoirs,* ed. E. B. Long. New York, 1952.

Graves, Robert. *Goodbye to All That.* London, 1929.

Grella, George. "James Bond, Culture Hero," *New Republic,* CL (30 May, 1964), 17–20.

Gummere, Francis B. "War and Romance," *Atlantic Monthly,* CXXVI (Oct. 1920), 490–96.

Guttman, Allen. *The Wound in the Heart: America and the Spanish Civil War.* New York, 1962.

Hackett, Alice Payne. *Seventy Years of Bestsellers, 1895–1965.* New York, 1968.

Haines, William. *Command Decision.* Boston, 1947.

Harris, Mark. *Something about a Soldier.* New York, 1957.

Hart, James D. *The Popular Book.* Berkeley, 1950.

Hasek, Jaroslav. *The Good Soldier Schweik,* trans. Paul Selver, il. Joseph Lada. London, 1930.

"Hassel, Sven," pseud. *The Legion of the Damned,* trans. Maurice Michael. Toronto, 1957.

Hayes, Alfred. *The Girl on the Via Flaminia.* Harmondsworth, 1957.

Hayford, Harrison, ed. *The Somers Mutiny Affair.* Englewood Cliffs, 1959.

Heggen, Thomas. *Mr. Roberts.* Boston, 1946.

Heller, Joseph. *Catch-22.* New York, 1962.
Hemingway, Ernest. *A Farewell to Arms.* New York, 1929.
———. *For Whom the Bell Tolls.* New York, 1940.
———. *In Our Time.* New York, 1930.
Hersey, John. *A Bell for Adano.* New York, 1944.
———. *Into the Valley: A Skirmish of the Marines.* New York, 1943.
———. *The War Lover.* New York, 1959.
Hoffman, Frederick J. *The Twenties: American Writing in the Post-War Decade.* New York, 1949.
Hofstadter, Richard. "Manifest Destiny and the Philippines," in *Crisis in America,* ed. Daniel Aaron. New York, 1952.
Hook, Sidney, et al. "Western Values and Total War," *Commentary,* XXXII (Oct. 1961), 277–304.
Hostovsky, Egon. *The Lonely Rebels.* New York, 1951.
Howard, Leon. *Herman Melville, a Biography.* Berkeley, 1951.
Huie, William Bradford. *The Execution of Private Slovik.* New York, 1954.
Huntington, Samuel P. *Changing Patterns of Military Politics.* New York, 1962.
———, et al. "No More Viet Nams? A Symposium," *Atlantic,* CCXXII (Nov. 1968), 99–116.
———. "Power, Expertise and the Military Profession," in *The Professions in America,* ed. K. S. Lynn. Boston, 1965, pp. 131–53.
———. *The Soldier and the State: The Theory and Politics of Civil-Military Relations.* Cambridge, Mass., 1957.
Janowitz, Morris. "Military Elites and the Study of War," in *War: Studies from Psychology, Sociology, and Anthropology,* eds. Leon Bramson and G. Goethals. New York, 1964, pp. 337–49.
———. *The Professional Soldier: A Social and Political Portrait.* Glencoe, Ill., 1960.
Jarrell, Randall. *Selected Poems.* New York, 1964.
Johnson, Gerald W. *Incredible Tale: The Odyssey of the Average American in the Last Half Century.* New York, 1950.
Johnson, Joseph E. "World Peace," in *Challenge to American Life,* ed. Andrew S. Berky. New York, 1956, pp. 105–26.
Jonas, Manfred. *Isolationism in America, 1935–1941.* Ithaca, 1966.
Jones, David. *In Parenthesis.* London, 1937.
Jones, Ernest. *Essays in Applied Psychoanalysis.* London, 1951.
Jones, James. *From Here to Eternity.* New York, 1951.
———. *The Thin Red Line.* New York, 1962.
Juenger, Ernst. *Storm of Steel,* trans. B. Creighton, with intro. by R. H. Mottram. London, 1929.
Karl, Frederick R. "Joseph Heller's *Catch-22:* Only Fools Walk in Darkness," in *Contemporary American Novelists,* ed. Harry T. Moore. Carbondale, 1964, pp. 134–42.
Kaufman, William W. *The McNamara Strategy.* New York, 1964.
Kazin, Alfred. "The Jew as Modern American Writer," in *Commentary Reader,* ed. Norman Podhoretz, New York, 1966, pp. xv–xxv.
———. "The Mindless Young Militants," *Commentary,* VI (1948), 495–501.
———. *On Native Grounds.* New York, 1942.
Keefe, Frederick. *The Investigating Officer.* New York, 1966.
Kirst, Helmut. *Forward, Gunner Asch,* trans. Robert Kee. Boston, 1956.
Kluckhohn, Clyde. "The Evolution of Contemporary American Values," *Daedalus,* LXXXVII (Spring 1958), 77–109.
Kris, Ernst, and Nathan Leites. "Trends in Twentieth Century Propaganda," in *Reader in Public Opinion and Communications,* eds. Ber-

nard Berelson and Morris Janowitz, enl. ed. Glencoe, Ill., 1953, pp. 278–88.

La Farge, Christopher. "Mickey Spillane and His Bloody Hammer," *Saturday Review,* XXXVII (6 Nov., 1954), 11–12, 54–59.

Lerner, Daniel. *Sykewar: Psychological Warfare against Germany, D-Day to V-E Day.* South Norwalk, Conn., 1949.

Lippard, Lucy R., ed. *Pop Art.* London, 1966.

Lively, Robert A. *Fiction Fights the Civil War.* Chapel Hill, 1957.

Löhrke, Eugene. *Armageddon: The World War in Literature.* New York, 1930.

Loveman, Amy. "Then and Now," *Saturday Review,* XXVII (7 Sep., 1940), 8.

Lowry, Robert. *Casualty.* Norfolk, Conn., 1946.

McAfee, Helen. "The Literature of Disillusion," *Atlantic Monthly,* CXXXII (Aug. 1923), 225–34.

McCook, Daniel. "The Second Division at Shiloh," *Harper's,* XXVIII (May 1864), 831.

McCormick, John. *Catastrophe and Imagination.* New York, 1957.

MacDonald, C. B. "Novels of World War II," *Military Affairs,* XIII (1949), 42–46.

MacLeish, Archibald. "Lines for an Interment," *New Republic,* LXXVI (20 Sep., 1933), 159.

Mahan, Alfred T. *The Influence of Sea Power upon History, 1660–1783,* 8th ed. London, n.d.

Mailer, Norman. *The Armies of the Night.* New York, 1968.

———. *The Naked and the Dead.* New York, 1948.

———. "Some Children of the Goddess," *Esquire,* LX (July 1963), 63–69.

———. *Why Are We in Viet Nam?* New York, 1967.

Marcuse, Ludwig. "The Oldest Younger Generation," trans. Willard R. Trask, *Partisan Review,* XIX (Mar. 1952), 211–16.

Marquand, John. *Melville Goodwin, U.S.A.* Boston, 1951.

———. *So Little Time.* Boston, 1943.

Matthews, Allen. *Assault.* New York, 1947.

Maurois, André. *Les discours du docteur O'Grady.* Paris, 1927.

———. *The New Freedom to the New Frontier: A History of the U.S.A. from Wilson to Kennedy,* trans. Patrick O'Brian. London, 1964.

May, Ernest R. *Imperial Democracy: The Emergence of America as a Great Power.* New York, 1961.

Melville, Herman. *Billy Budd.* New York, 1962.

Michener, James. *The Bridges at Toko-ri.* New York, 1952.

———. *Tales of the South Pacific.* Toronto, 1947.

Miller, Merle. *That Winter.* New York, 1948.

Millis, Walter. *Arms and Men: A Study in American Military History.* New York, 1956.

———. *Road to War.* Boston, 1935.

Mills, C. Wright. *The Power Elite.* New York, 1956.

Morison, Samuel E. *The Oxford History of the American People.* New York, 1965.

Muggeridge, Malcolm. "James Bond: The Myth and Its Master," *Observer* (30 May, 1965), p. 21.

Mumford, Lewis. *The City in History.* New York, 1961.

———. *The Golden Day.* New York, 1926.

Muste, John W. "Better to Die Laughing: The War Novels of Joseph Heller and John Ashmead," *Critique,* V (Fall 1962), 16–27.

Niebuhr, Reinhold. *The Irony of American History.* New York, 1952.

Opitz, Karl Ludwig. *The General,* trans. Constantine Fitzgibbon. New York, 1957.

Packard, Vance. *The Pyramid Climbers.* Harmondsworth, 1968.

Parrington, Vernon. *The Beginnings of Critical Realism in America,* vol. III, *Main Currents in American Thought.* New York, 1930.

Peterson, H. C. *Propaganda for War.* Norman, Okla., 1939.

Phillips, William. "What Happened in the Thirties," in *Commentary Reader,* ed. Norman Podhoretz. New York, 1966, pp. 752–63.

Pinsker, Sanford. "Heller's *Catch-22:* The Protest of a 'Puer Eternis,'" *Critque,* VII (Winter 1964), 150–62.

Plivier, Theodore. *Stalingrad,* trans. Richard and Clara Winston. New York, 1964.

Podhoretz, Norman. *Doings and Undoings: The Fifties and After in American Writing.* London, 1965.

Pratt, Julius W. "The Business Attitude toward the Spanish-American War," in *Understanding the American Past,* ed. Edward N. Saveth. New York, 1954, pp. 406–21.

——. "The 'Large Policy' of 1898," in *Recent America,* ed. S. Fine. New York, 1962, pp. 4–23.

Pritchett, V. S. "American Soldiers," *New Statesman,* LXV (8 Feb., 1963), 207.

Putney, S., and R. Middleton. "Some Factors Associated with Student Acceptance or Rejection of War," *American Sociological Review,* XXVII (Oct. 1962), 655–67.

Pyle, Ernie. *Here Is Your War.* New York, 1943.

Rahv, Philip. "The Cult of Experience in American Writing," *Partisan Review,* VII (1940), 412–24.

——. "In Retrospect," in *Partisan Review Anthology,* eds. William Phillips and Philip Rahv. London, 1962.

Ramsey, Vance. "From Here to Absurdity: Heller's *Catch-22,*" in *Seven Contemporary Authors,* ed. Thomas B. Whitbread. Austin, 1966, pp. 97–118.

Rascoe, Burton. "What They Read during the Last War," *Saturday Review,* XX (23 Sep. 1939), 3–4, 13–16.

Remarque, Erich Maria. *All Quiet on the Western Front,* trans. A. W. Wheens. London, 1929.

Remenyi, Joseph. "The Psychology of War Literature," *Sewanee Review,* LII (1944), 137–47.

Rolo, Charles J. "Simenon and Spillane: The Metaphysics of Murder for the Millions," *New World Writing,* I (1952), 234–45.

Roosevelt, Theodore. "A. T. Mahan's *The Influence of Sea Power upon History,*" *Atlantic,* LXVI (Oct. 1890), 563–67.

Ropp, Theodore. *War in the Western World.* Durham, N.C., 1959.

Rublowsky, John. *Pop Art: Images of the American Dream.* Camden, N.J., 1965.

Rugoff, Milton. "Dos Passos, Novelist of Our Time," *Sewanee Review,* XLIX (1941), 453–68.

Santayana, George. *Character and Opinion in the United States.* Garden City, 1956.

Schlesinger, Arthur M., Jr. *A Thousand Days: John F. Kennedy in the White House.* Boston, 1965.

Sewall, Richard B. *The Vision of Tragedy.* New Haven, 1965.

Shannon, David A. *Between the Wars: America, 1919–1941.* New York, 1965.

Shaw, Irwin. *The Young Lions.* New York, 1948.

Sherwood, Robert E. *Roosevelt and Hopkins: An Intimate History,* rev. ed. New York, 1950.

Smith, Louis. *American Democracy and Military Power: A Study of Civil Control of the Military Power in the United States.* Chicago, 1951.

Smith, R. H. "A Review: *Catch-22*" in *The American Reading Public,* ed. R. H. Smith. New York, 1964, pp. 234–47.

Social Service Research Council. Committee on Civil-Military Relations Research. *Civil-Military Relations: An Annotated Bibliography, 1940–1952.* New York, 1954.

Sorensen, Theodore. *Kennedy.* London, 1966.

Spiller, Robert E., et al., eds. *A Literary History of the United States,* 3rd ed. rev. New York, 1963.

Sprout, Harold, and Margaret Sprout. *The Rise of American Naval Power, 1776–1918.* Princeton, 1945.

Stegner, Wallace. "The Mounties at Fort Walsh," in *Essay,* ed. Hans P. Guth. Belmont, Calif., 1962, pp. 215–23.

Stevens, James. *Mattock.* New York, 1927.

Stockton, Frank. *The Great War Syndicate.* New York, 1889.

Strausz-Hupé, Robert. "The Disarmament Delusion," in *The Debate over Thermonuclear Strategy,* ed. A. I. Waskow. Boston, 1965, pp. 82–90.

Streeter, Edward. *Dere Mable.* New York, 1918.

Styron, William. *The Long March.* New York, 1953.

———. "My Generation," *Esquire,* LXX (Oct. 1968), 122–24.

Thomas, Hugh. *The Spanish Civil War.* Harmondsworth, 1968.

Thompson, Kenneth W. "Nuclear Weapons: Four Crucial Questions," in *Conflict and Cooperation among Nations,* ed. I. Duchacek. New York, 1960, pp. 443–50.

Tocqueville, Alexis de. *Democracy in America,* trans. Henry Reeve, with intro. by H. S. Commager. London, 1946.

Toynbee, Arnold. "The Changes in the United States Position and Outlook as a World Power during the Last Half-Century," in *Man, Science, Learning and Education,* ed. S. W. Higginbotham. Houston, 1963, pp. 1–20.

Traina, Richard P. *American Diplomacy and the Spanish Civil War.* Bloomington, Ind., 1968.

Truman, Harry S. *Memoirs,* 2 vols. New York, 1956.

Trumbo, Dalton. *Johnny Got His Gun.* New York, 1939.

Turner, E. S. "Boy, Did We Clobber the Mahrattas!" *Punch,* CCLIV (6 Mar., 1968), 337–39.

Twain, Mark. *A Connecticut Yankee in King Arthur's Court.* New York, 1917.

"The Two Presidents," *Nation,* CCVIII (23 June, 1969), 778.

Uris, Leon. *Battle Cry.* New York, 1953.

Vagts, Alfred. *A History of Militarism, Civilian and Military.* Greenwich, Conn. 1959.

Van Alstyne, Richard W. *American Diplomacy in Action.* Stanford, 1947.

Van Doren, Mark. "Post-War: The Literary Twenties," *Harper's,* CLXXIII (1936), 148–56.

Van Nostrand, Albert. *The Denatured Novel.* New York, 1960.

Volpe, Edmund L. "James Jones—Norman Mailer," in *Contemporary American Novelists,* ed. Harry T. Moore. Carbondale, Ill., 1964, pp. 106–19.

Vonnegut, Kurt. *Mother Night.* New York, 1967.

Vonnegut, Kurt. *Player Piano*. London, 1969.

Wakefield, Dan. "Supernation at Peace and War," *Atlantic*, CCXXI (Mar. 1968), 39–105.

Waldmeir, Joseph J. "Ideological Aspects of the American Novels of World War II." Ph.D. dissertation, Michigan State Univ., 1959.

"War's Reaction on Literature," *Nation*, XCIX (31 Dec., 1914), 765.

Waskow, A. I. ed. *The Debate Over Thermonuclear Strategy*. Boston, 1965.

Wecter, Dixon. *When Johnny Comes Marching Home*. New York, 1944.

Weigley, Russell F. *Towards an American Army*. New York, 1962.

Wharton, Edith. *The Marne*. New York, 1918.

———. *A Son at the Front*. New York, 1923.

Whelpley, James Davenport. "America and the European War," *Fortnightly Review*, XCVI (Sep. 1914), 482.

Wilkinson, Clennell. "Back to All That," *London Mercury*, XXII (1930), 539–46.

———. "Recent War Books," *London Mercury*, XXI (1930), 236–42.

Williams, T. Harry. *Americans at War*. Baton Rouge, 1960.

Wilson, Edmund. *The Shores of Light: A Literary Chronicle of the Twenties and Thirties*. New York, 1961.

Woodcock, George. "The Thirties and the Sixties," *Saturday Night*, LXXXIV (Dec. 1969), 33–37.

Woodward, C. Vann. "The Age of Reinterpretation," *American Historical Review*, LXVI (Oct. 1960), 1–19.

———. Review of Henry F. May's *The End of American Innocence: A Study of the First Years of Our Own Time, 1912–1917*. *American Historical Review*, LXV (Apr. 1960), 637–38.

Wouk, Herman. *The Caine Mutiny*. New York, 1951.

Wylie, Philip. *Tomorrow!* New York, 1954.

Yeats, William Butler. *The Collected Poems*. London, 1952.

Zentner, H. "Morale," *American Sociological Review*, XVI (June 1951), 297–310.

Zweig, Arnold. *The Case of Sergeant Grischa*, trans. Eric Sutton. London, 1928.

INDEX